Troubled Debt Restructuring
An Alternative to Bankruptcy?

Research for Business Decisions, No. 81

Richard N. Farmer, Series Editor

Professor of International Business
Indiana University

Other Titles in This Series

Troubled Debt Restructuring
An Alternative to Bankruptcy?

by
John G. Hamer

UMI RESEARCH PRESS
Ann Arbor, Michigan

Produced and distributed by
UMI Research Press
an imprint of
University Microfilms International
A Xerox Information Resources Company
Ann Arbor, Michigan 48106

Library of Congress Cataloging in Publication Data

Hamer, John G., (John Gwenffrud), 1955-
Troubled debt restructuring.

(Research for business decisions ; no. 81)
Revision of thesis (Ph. D.)—Texas A & M
University, 1983.
Bibliography: p.
Includes index.
1. Corporate debt.   2. Bankruptcy—Fore-
casting—Mathematical models.   I. Title.
II. Series.
HG4028.D3H27   1985   332.7   85-16503
ISBN 0-8357-1716-X (alk. paper)

Contents

Acknowledgments

I am indebted to numerous people for their assistance and support while writing this book. For their technical support, James Benjamin, Gary Giroux, Peter Rose, and James Matis, all of Texas A&M University, were invaluable. The administration at the University of Lowell provided a great amount of assistance. Other people who have provided support include Roger Bailey, Clairmont Carter, Jacqueline Kozlowski, Mark Krikorian, Steven Morin, Patricia Ouellette, Lynn Thomas, Daniel Verreault, Kathryn Verreault, Jeffrey Welch, and JoAnne Williams.

1

Introduction

For several years, bankruptcy has been a topic of interest to researchers in the areas of both accounting and finance. When a firm is in financial difficulty, its only recourse may be to file for bankruptcy under the National Bankruptcy Act. Under this act, the firm may be able to reorganize and become a going concern again or may be forced into liquidation. Bankruptcy is the last resort for financially troubled firms.

Since bankruptcy is such an important event, most studies have attempted to detect firms which would eventually file for bankruptcy. There are two theories concerning bankruptcy. One theory states that the onset of bankruptcy may be very quick so that no indicators can predict bankruptcy before it actually occurs. The other theory considers bankruptcy to be a long-term process. In the latter case, there may be indicators which predict the bankruptcy of a given firm at some point in the future.

It is from this latter view that several bankruptcy models have been developed in an effort to predict the future status of firms as bankrupt or nonbankrupt. In most of these studies, the variables chosen to characterize a sample of firms as bankrupt or nonbankrupt have been financial ratios. In other words, troubled firms should have significantly different financial ratios than healthy firms.

Before a firm reaches the point of bankruptcy, there may be several alternatives open to it to reverse its troubled position and prevent bankruptcy. One alternative is to undergo troubled debt restructuring (TDR) where, if the creditors agree, the firm is able to either reduce or extend its debt, or both. In this book several aspects of TDRs are studied. Using a sample of TDR firms, tests are first conducted to determine if these firms are classified as bankrupt or nonbankrupt prior to debt restructuring. A discriminant bankruptcy model is developed similar to those developed by others (Altman, 1977; Rose and Giroux, 1980). Second, the TDR sample is tested after restructuring to determine if, in fact, the firms reverse their troubled positions and become profitable. The characteristics of these firms are analyzed to determine whether or not they are progressing through a process that usually results in bankruptcy. If not, the restructuring will have occurred with no indications of future financial problems. Since this is the first empirical study pertaining to TDRs, the results should prove quite useful for future research.

When a firm becomes unable to pay its debts, the TDR alternative has two possible results. First, the TDR may make it possible for the firm to pay its debts and continue to function as a going concern. Alternatively, the TDR may have no effect on the failure process; therefore, the firm soon faces loan default, bankruptcy, and possible liquidation. This study will determine if the majority of the TDR firms show signs of financial difficulty before TDR takes place. Also, after TDR, the financial direction that these firms take will be observed. These firms can either strengthen, remain the same, or worsen.

The research questions may be restated as follows: Is there evidence that recourse to a TDR is part of the failure process? In other words, prior to restructuring, do TDR firms possess the characteristics of bankrupt or nonbankrupt firms? Has TDR aided troubled firms in reversing their progression through the failure process? In other words, after restructuring, do the characteristics of the TDR firms differ from what they were before restructuring? Or do they maintain the same characteristics as before? And were these characteristics similar to those of either bankrupt or nonbankrupt firms? Are these firms able to settle their debt? Finally, are these firms able to continue to function as going concerns?

The following hypotheses will be tested to answer the above questions:

(One-sided)

1. H0: The difference in mean Z scores before TDR from one year
       to the next for the TDR firms is less than or equal to zero.
   H1: The difference in mean Z scores before TDR from one year
       to the next for the TDR firms is greater than zero.

(Two-sided)

2. H0: The difference in mean Z scores after TDR from one year to
       the next for the TDR firms is zero.
   H1: The difference in mean Z scores after TDR from one year to
       the next for the TDR firms is not zero.

The Z score is computed by the discriminant function to determine the financial position of each firm. High positive Z scores represent profitable firms while negative Z scores represent unprofitable ones. In the first hypothesis, if Z scores are decreasing prior to TDR, then the difference in Z scores for each firm over a one-year period should be positive. In the second hypothesis, if Z scores are changing (either positively or negatively), then the difference between Z scores for each firm over a one-year period should not be equal to zero. If the firm's financial condition continues to worsen, the differences in Z scores should be positive. If the firm's financial condition, in fact, becomes stronger, the differences in Z scores should be negative.

Next, we wish to test the null hypothesis that the proportion of TDR firms classified as bankrupt or nonbankrupt remains the same for each year prior to TDR and each year after TDR. We let p1 be the proportion of TDR firms which are classified as bankrupt in one year and p2 be the proportion of TDR firms which are classified as bankrupt in the next year. We may state the null and alternative hypotheses symbolically as follows (Daniel, 1978):

3. H0: $p1 = p2$ or $p1 - p2 = 0$,   H1: $p1 \neq p2$ or $p1 - p2 \neq 0$
4. H0: $M = M0$,   H1: $M \neq M0$ where M is the firm's mean scores and M0 is the hypothesized median of Z scores.

These hypotheses will be tested for several years. First they will be tested for each year up to three years prior to TDR. Then they will be tested for each year up to three years after the TDR.

5. H0: The distribution of Z scores of the TDR firms is homogeneous.
   H1: The distribution of Z scores of TDR firms is not homogeneous.

The above hypothesis should indicate whether the TDR firms are homogeneous in their bankrupt or nonbankrupt characteristics or if a dichotomy exists within the sample. This is important for several reasons. First, testing of this hypothesis prior to TDR will indicate if the TDR firms are similar to bankrupt firms. Testing of this hypothesis after TDR will indicate whether or not these firms retain the same status or whether their financial positions change so that they are similar to nonbankrupt firms.

Multiple discriminant analysis (MDA) will be used to develop a bankruptcy prediction model. The discriminant model developed will be similar to those developed in the past and will use those variables found to be most predictive. A sample of bankrupt and nonbankrupt firms will be used to develop this model. Next, a sample of firms will be evaluated before they entered TDR using the bankruptcy model. If the firms were having financial difficulties prior to TDR, the model may classify them as being bankrupt firms. If not, they will be classified as nonbankrupt firms. After the TDR, these same firms (where data are available) will be evaluated again using this same model. If TDR has been effective in turning these firms around, the model may then classify a significant number of them as nonbankrupt.

Economic Conditions of the United States

The economic conditions of the nation have a major effect on the operations of a business. There have been major efforts by government to reduce inflation and unemployment while achieving economic growth. Because business failures have more than tripled since 1981 it is useful to look at some of the economic statistics of the time period. The increase in business failures may vary inversely with economic conditions. As inflation, interest rates, and unemployment rise, the number of business failures rises (*Annual Report*, Federal Reserve Bank of New York, 1982).

After the oil crisis in 1973, the country entered into a recessionary period. Throughout the mid 1970s, the rate of inflation and unemployment decreased. The following table contains economic data for the United States from 1972 to 1981.

Year	1972	1973	1974	1975	1976
GNP (Billions)	$1185.9	$1326.4	$1434.2	$1549.2	$1718.0
Unemployment Rate	4.9	4.4	5.2	7.9	5.9
Discount Rate	4.5	7.5	7.75	6.0	5.25
Inflation Rate	6.12	8.46	11.24	6.53	4.56

Year	1977	1978	1979	1980	1981
GNP (Billions)	$1918.3	$2163.9	$2417.8	$2633.1	$2937.7
Unemployment Rate	7.0	6.2	6.1	7.6	8.3
Discount Rate	6.0	9.5	12.0	12.87	13.41
Inflation Rate	6.16	8.45	12.31	10.81	8.06

In the late 1970s, the rate of economic growth increased. Unemployment also dropped significantly to less than six percent in 1976. However, inflation increased in the late 1970s. The major cause of increased inflation was a shortage of raw materials, which caused poor productivity in the nation's industry (*Economic Report of the President*, 1980).

In 1979, oil prices more than doubled. Inflation was still on the rise at 12.31 percent while the unemployment rate remained at 6 percent. The Federal Reserve's discount rate was rising at this time. Investment decreased. The discount rate reached a new high of 13.41 percent in 1981.

The Carter Administration ended in 1980 with an inflation rate of 10.81 percent. While government spending reduced unemployment during this period, individuals and businesses were suffering from the high inflation and interest rates. Plans for economic recovery began in 1981 with a decrease in government spending, a decrease in the federal income tax rates, and deregulation. It was hoped that this plan would reduce inflation, interest rates, and unemployment, while stimulating business investment and productivity.

As of December 1982, inflation had been substantially reduced to 5 percent. The discount rate at this time had dropped to 11.02 percent. However, the GNP had shown no evidence that the business segment had increased investment. Unemployment had risen to 10.7 percent.

The economic recovery plans of the 1980s have been considered partially successful by some people. Interest rates have declined, which enables firms to borrow funds more cheaply. This may increase business investment and production and lead to reduced unemployment and economic growth. However, the new concerns and fears of the people are related to unemployment.

In summary, the economy in the United States from 1972 to 1982 experienced several adverse changes. In general, interest rates and unemployment increased over this ten-year period. The discount rate reached its peak in 1979 and began to decline thereafter. This economic turmoil, although not solely responsible, had a major effect on the increasing rate of bankruptcies in the United States (Argenti, 1976). In 1979, there were 7,757 business failures in which companies filed for bankruptcy. This number increased each year, to 25,346 in 1982 (*Annual Report,* Federal Reserve Bank of New York, 1982). Below is a summary showing the number of business failures in the United States over the past ten years.

Year	Number of Business Failures	Percent Change
1973	9,571	-
1974	10,046	4.96%
1975	11,629	15.76%
1976	9,851	-18.05%
1977	7,988	-18.91%
1978	6,720	-15.87%
1979	7,757	15.43%
1980	11,782	51.89%
1981	17,217	46.13%
1982	25,346	47.21%

Source: Adapted from the *Annual Report,* Federal Reserve Bank of New York, 1982

The state of the general economy and the probability of bankruptcy vary inversely. As firms are subject to an economic turndown, they tend to become less profitable and financially worse off, often succumbing to bankruptcy. As a result, interest in TDRs rose, which led to the issuance of *FASB Statement No.*

15 in 1977 (Kolins, 1977). The decline in the economy caused an increased interest in business failures and troubled debt restructurings.

Relevance of This Study

No empirical studies thus far have attempted to determine the effects of TDR on troubled firms. Studies in the TDR area have been limited to summaries of, and how to apply, a troubled debt restructuring. Since debt restructuring may not have been a common occurrence, data may have been difficult to obtain, but with the data available since disclosure has been required under *FASB Statement No. 15*, sufficient information could be obtained for this study once it was determined that a sufficient number of firms had implemented TDR to obtain an acceptable sample size. A sample of 60 TDR firms was established.

Research in the bankruptcy area has resulted in empirical models which predict and classify bankruptcy before the fact. These models are well known and widely accepted (Altman et al., 1977; Rose and Giroux, 1980). While these models consider factors such as liquidity, profitability, leverage, and other factors, they do not consider TDR, which may be a step in the failure process.

There have also been theoretical models which attempt to predict the probability of failure (Scott, 1979), though only a few have appeared to date. These studies have attempted to explain the results obtained from the empirical studies. Scott (1981) has found many factors in common between the theoretical and empirical models. The common factors or ratios are EBIT (earnings before interest and taxes)/total interest payments, EBIT/TA (total assets), and common equity/total capital.

All the empirical bankruptcy studies of the past have been ex-post in nature. In other words, the prediction models were developed from firms which had already filed for bankruptcy. A TDR is a pre-bankruptcy event. In this study, the TDR sample will be evaluated using a discriminant model which is ex-post in nature. Since the concepts of TDR and bankruptcy are closely related, tying the two together is pertinent to research in this area, and the results of this study may be useful in future research in the development of an ex-ante (before bankruptcy) bankruptcy model.

The results of the study could prove useful to debtors, creditors, and investors. Although each firm is different, the general conclusions drawn from this study could influence the decision-making process concerning TDRs. If TDRs are shown to have helped troubled firms, future troubled firms may make greater efforts to implement a TDR. Creditors could become more flexible in granting TDRs or more lenient in establishing the terms of a TDR.

Conversely, if TDRs have not proven to be successful, troubled firms may not view the TDR as a "way out of the tunnel." These firms may simply proceed to the next step, bankruptcy, or they may choose another alternative, such as a merger. Creditors may become more strict in granting TDRs if they have been unsuccessful in the past; creditors may also become more conservative in establishing the terms of a TDR.

The conclusions presented in this study may, on the other hand, not be strong enough to prove that TDRs are or are not a favorable alternative. Much additional research is needed in this area which may support or not support the implementation of TDRs.

Limitations

There are several limitations to this study. The main limitation is that factors other than debt restructuring may have an impact on the restructured firm. For example, the state of the economy may affect a particular firm's position. If a firm has restructured its debt and economic conditions for the firm's industry subsequently improve, what explanation should be given for the firm's recovery? By using a sample of firms in different industries, the overall importance of these factors may be reduced, but it is impossible to totally isolate debt restructuring.

There are limitations when using MDA (multiple discriminant analysis). Ohlson (1980) cites a few:

1. There are certain statistical requirements imposed on the distributional properties of the predictors. For example, the variance-covariance matrices of the predictors should be the same for both groups (failed and non-failed firms); moreover, a requirement of normally distributed predictors certainly mitigates against the use of dummy independent variables. A violation of these conditions, it could perhaps be argued, is unimportant (or simply irrelevant) if the only purpose of the model is to develop a discriminating device.

MDA has been found to be a powerful test, even when these requirements are violated. Tests will determine the equality of the variance-covariance matrices and the normality of the predictors. The statistical package, MULDIS, computes the variance-covariance matrices.

2. The output of the application of an MDA model is a score which has little intuitive interpretation, since it is basically an ordinal ranking (discriminatory) device. For decision problems such that a misclassification structure is an inadequate description of the payoff partition, the score is not directly relevant. If, however, prior probabilities of the two groups are specified, then it is possible to derive posterior probabilities of failure. But, this Bayesian revision process will be invalid or lead to poor approximations unless the assumptions of normality, etc. are satisfied.
3. There are also certain problems related to the "matching" procedures which have typically been used in MDA. Failed and non-failed firms are matched according to criteria such as size and industry, and these tend to be somewhat arbitrary. It is by no means obvious what is really gained or lost by different matching procedures, including no matching at all. At the very least, it would seem to be more fruitful actually to include variables as predictors rather than to use them for matching purposes.

The TDR firms in this study will not be matched with any other firms. The firms will be compared with both the bankrupt and nonbankrupt samples to determine any similarities or dissimilarities. It is unknown at this point whether the TDR sample is a group separate from these two samples. The discriminant model will be developed by matching a sample of bankrupt and nonbankrupt firms. From this model, the TDR firms will be analyzed by their computed Z scores. The changes in these Z scores will detect the effects of TDR on these firms. Since this is essentially a comparison of Z scores within firms from one year to the next, any changes should reflect the firms' financial condition. When analyzed using the model, the dissimilarities between these firms and the bankrupt firms for which the model was developed may bias the results. Therefore, the predictive ability of the independent variables could differ between the original samples of failed and non-failed firms and the TDR firms. In other words, the model may not be the best model for analyzing TDR firms.

Industrial firms will be used to develop the discriminant model. The COMPUSTAT Industrial File will facilitate the data-gathering process. The TDR firms will be all those found by DISCLOSURE, Inc., so not all of the selected firms will be industrial firms. Some of these have been eliminated from the TDR sample. For example, commercial banks were deleted from the sample because the TDRs they reported were their customers', not their own. Since the sample is not a random sample but an entire population, the possibility exists that the results are biased. The industries in the TDR sample are similar to those of the COMPUSTAT firms. However, since DISCLOSURE, Inc. is the best source for the sample, it was used in this study.

Debt restructuring may prove effective for certain types of firms or firms experiencing certain types of difficulties. The model does not take into account why a firm is in financial difficulty, only that it is. Future research may need to concern itself with why a firm becomes a troubled firm. The leniency of terms of the TDR may also affect the financial outcome of the companies.

A final limitation of this study is the source of the TDR sample. As was mentioned above, the sample was obtained from DISCLOSURE, Inc. This service listed all publicly traded firms which reported debt restructuring in their published financial statements in 1982. Some of these firms, however, had restructured their debt several years previously. However, as noted in table 1 (see p. 28), eight of these firms had never entered into a TDR. Therefore DISCLOSURE, Inc. is not without its shortcomings. However, at this time it provides the most complete and reliable sample available.

2

Review of the Literature

This chapter is divided into two parts, the first of which contains a review of the limited literature pertaining to TDR. The chapter concludes with a summary and description of the bankruptcy literature.

Troubled Debt Restructuring

In June 1977, the Financial Accounting Standards Board (FASB) issued *FASB Statement No. 15*, "Accounting by Debtors and Creditors for Troubled Debt Restructurings." A troubled debt restructuring occurs "if the creditor for economic or legal reasons related to the debtor's financial difficulties grants a concession that it would not otherwise consider" (FASB, 1978). These arrangements are intended to keep the debtor from going into bankruptcy.

According to the FASB, a troubled debt restructuring may include, but is not limited to, one or any combination of the following:

a. Transfer from debtor to the creditor of receivables from third parties, real estate, or other assets to satisfy fully or partially a debt (including a transfer resulting from foreclosure or repossession).
b. Issuance or other granting of an equity interest to the creditor by the debtor to satisfy fully or partially a debt, unless the equity interest is granted pursuant to existing terms for converting the debt into an equity interest.
c. Modification of terms of a debt, such as one or a combination of:
   1. Reduction (absolute or contingent) of the stated interest rate for the remaining original life of the debt.
   2. Extension of the maturity date or dates at a stated interest rate lower than the current market rate for new debt with similar risk.
   3. Reduction (absolute or contingent) of the face amount or maturity amount of the debt as stated in the instrument or other agreement.
   4. Reduction (absolute or contingent) of accrued interest.

Troubled debt restructuring may result in a gain for the debtor if the amount to be repaid under the restructuring is less than the carrying value of the debt.

However, if the debtor must repay more than the carrying value of the debt, no gain or loss is recognized.

Information about any troubled debt restructuring must be disclosed in the body of the financial statements of a firm or in the footnotes. Disclosure must be made for the period of restructuring and any subsequent periods in which amounts contingently payable are included in the carrying amount of the restructured debt. Prior to this statement, no disclosure concerning TDR was necessary.

Although this study is concerned with TDR in general, all of the firms in the sample are ones which have implemented *FASB Statement No. 15*. Since no disclosure was required prior to the statement, the data needed for analysis were impossible to find for firms which did not disclose TDRs. The sample consists of all those publicly traded firms which disclosed a TDR in their 1981 financial statements. Some of these TDRs go back several years while others are current.

Since there have been no empirical TDR studies to date, the only TDR literature published is descriptive in nature. Although these are not research studies as such, a brief review of what has been published in the TDR area is presented below for completeness.

Norby (1976) cited large loan losses of banks and market losses on New York City bonds as stimulating interest in TDRs. As TDRs became more important, the AICPA showed interest in TDR accounting by banks. In 1975, the FASB issued an exposure draft dealing with TDRs and later withdrew it.

Hauge (1976) says that the concern over TDRs in the 1970s was the greatest since the 1930s. A discussion memorandum issued by the FASB in 1976 suggests the use of current value accounting, market values, and present value techniques in accounting for TDRs.

Hauge says that users and preparers of financial statements do not understand present value techniques, which were implemented in the discussion memorandum prior to the issuance of *FASB Statement No. 15*. Therefore the discussion memorandum should be questioned. In the past, TDRs did not affect financial statements. But a new accounting method may be detrimental to business, since required disclosure can affect investors' and creditors' perceptions and even stock prices.

New methods of accounting for TDRs could change the manner in which creditors extend credit, according to Hauge. Also, using present value techniques, earnings of banks could become distorted. For example, if banks do not like the new methods of accounting for TDRs, they might be more hesitant to grant them. Other creditors could become more stringent in granting credit. As a result, small and marginal businesses might find a reduction of credit availability.

Phillips (1977) discusses TDRs and real estate investment trusts. He notes that several types of TDRs had been used prior to *FASB Statement No. 15*. Many of these types are described in *FASB Statement No. 15*. He concludes by summarizing the 1976 exposure draft issued by the FASB and acknowledges its leniency in accounting for TDRs. The exposure draft essentially allows the creditor to structure the TDR as he wishes.

The relevant literature pertaining to *FASB Statement No. 15* has been mostly descriptive in nature. Beresford and Neary (1977) state that in most cases no gain or loss will be recognized by debtors and creditors in a debt restructuring. However, in a situation where the future cash flows of interest and principal to be repaid by the debtor are less than the carrying amount of the debt before the restructuring, the debtor will recognize a gain and the creditor will recognize a loss.

Hiltner and Oien (1978) define a troubled debt restructuring and list the possible forms a debt restructuring may take as defined in *FASB Statement No. 15.* They present two flowcharts for debt restructuring; these show what courses of action are available to creditors and debtors. The flowcharts follow the order of accounting operations necessary when implementing *FASB Statement No. 15.* They start with loan default, the alternative choices allowed under a TDR, and the results that may occur. There is no guarantee that a TDR will enable a firm to operate profitably again.

Kolins (1977) discusses the guidelines for debt restructuring as outlined in *FASB Statement No. 15,* and provides a brief numerical example. He also points out that any gain to be recognized by the debtor, if material, should be classified as an extraordinary gain.

Ratcliffe and Raiborn (1981) outline *FASB Statement No. 15* for debtors, including the appropriate disclosure requirements. Ratcliffe and Munter (1980) outline *FASB Statement No. 15* for creditors, including the appropriate disclosure requirements.

For debtors, the disclosure requirements include a description of the change(s), any gain to be recognized (with tax effect), per-share amount of gain (net of tax), aggregate gain or loss recognized during the period attributable to asset transfers, and the extent to which any contingent payments are included in the carrying amount of restructured payables (Ratcliffe and Raiborn, 1981).

For creditors, the disclosure requirements include outstanding receivables whose terms have been modified by major category, the aggregate recorded investment, the gross interest income foregone during the period through restructuring the receivable, and the amount of interest income on those receivables included in income for the period. The amount of any commitments to lend additional funds to troubled debtors whose restructured receivables have not been satisfied must also be disclosed (Ratcliffe and Munter, 1980).

Bankruptcy

Business failure has been a topic of great interest over the past 15 years. If early-warning signs of business failure can be pinpointed, it is possible that the number of future business failures may be substantially reduced. If a troubled firm can be made aware of its impending failure, it may be able to take some appropriate steps to reverse its troubled situation. Several types of variables which indicate failure have already been studied.

Defining business failure is not a simple task. Previous studies have chosen different definitions. Examples include operating results below expectations, net loss and nonpayment of dividends, net loss and negative cash flows, deteriorating results year after year, loan default, Chapter X or Chapter XI bankruptcy, and liquidation (Rose and Giroux, 1980). A firm may experience negative cash flows for a few years but manage to recover. Also, a firm may file bankruptcy under Chapter XI of the Bankruptcy Code, but if the firm (debtor) can work out a suitable arrangement with its creditors, it may recover and continue as a profitable firm.

Bankruptcy Continuum

Giroux and Wiggins (1983) developed a bankruptcy continuum, as presented in figure 1. In this model, the pattern begins with the first signs of trouble for a firm and continues all the way through liquidation. The first four indicators—poor operating results, net loss, nonpayment of dividends, and negative cash flows— are the early symptoms of potential distress. Poor operating results are trouble spots which occur when a firm can no longer carry out its goals due to its financial position (e.g., net loss, nonpayment of dividends). However, if operating results deteriorate year after year, the final outcome is likely to be loan default and/or bankruptcy. If reorganization under the bankruptcy law is ineffective, the firm may have to liquidate.

Some specific events which may occur, indicating future bankruptcy, have been suggested by Giroux and Wiggins' model. Under this bankruptcy continuum, net loss, nonpayment of dividends, negative cash flows, deteriorating results, and loan default are all part of this long-term process. In the past, variables such as financial ratios have been used to measure this process in prediction models. Different variables have been used in an attempt to predict bankruptcy. Generally, there has been overall agreement that variables do exist which predict bankruptcy; however, there has not been full agreement as to which specific variables should be used.

When a firm experiences deteriorating results, which can be defined as lower levels of income year after year or increases in losses from year to year, there are several possible outcomes. First, a firm may be able to turn itself around and become profitable again due to better management or better economic conditions. Second, a firm may enter into a merger with a profitable firm in order to avoid loan default and possible bankruptcy. Third, it may enter into a troubled debt restructuring in an effort to reduce or delay its debt. Fourth, if a firm has defaulted on a loan, it may then attempt to enter into a TDR in order to turn its position around again. Finally, the firm may reorganize under the National Bankruptcy Act in order to become a going concern again. While none of these alternatives will ensure a troubled firm relief, they are routes which, if taken, may help the firm to avoid being forced into liquidation.

Figure 1
Spectrum of Business Failure Events

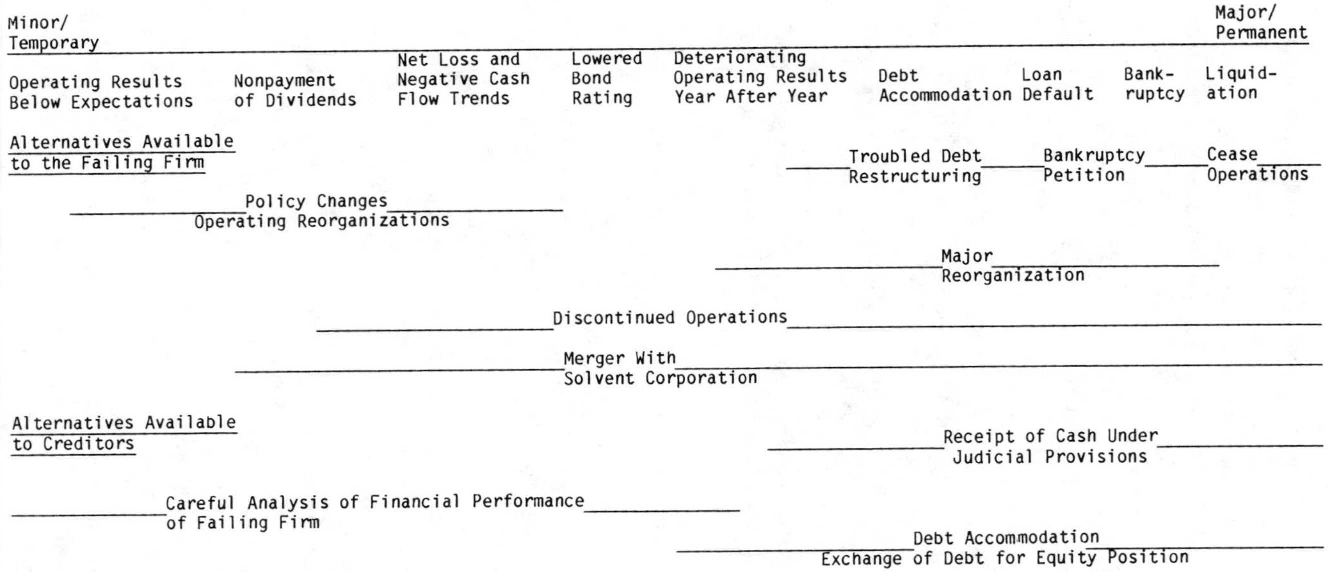

Minor/Temporary								Major/Permanent
Operating Results Below Expectations	Nonpayment of Dividends	Net Loss and Negative Cash Flow Trends	Lowered Bond Rating	Deteriorating Operating Results Year After Year	Debt Accommodation	Loan Default	Bankruptcy Petition	Bankruptcy	Liquidation	Cease Operations

Alternatives Available
to the Failing Firm

Policy Changes
Operating Reorganizations

Discontinued Operations

Merger With
Solvent Corporation

Troubled Debt
Restructuring ____ Bankruptcy Petition

Major
Reorganization

Alternatives Available
to Creditors

Careful Analysis of Financial Performance
of Failing Firm

Receipt of Cash Under
Judicial Provisions

Debt Accommodation
Exchange of Debt for Equity Position

Source: Adapted from Giroux and Wiggins, 1983

When a firm is unable to pay its debts, it may enter into an agreement with its creditors to change the terms of its debt. However, the creditors of the firm must agree to a TDR in order for it to be implemented. Although the creditors always make the final decisions, the terms of the TDR must be mutually agreed upon between the debtors and creditors. Also, these terms must follow the guidelines of *FASB Statement No. 15.*

The firm may want to enter into this TDR in order to avoid default and possible bankruptcy. As a result of the TDR, the firm may turn around and become a profitable concern again or it may still head toward bankruptcy. It is the hope of the firm that the TDR will result in the settlement of debts and long-run profitability and liquidity.

Likewise, when a creditor agrees to a TDR, the creditor wants the troubled firm to meet its obligations under the TDR. If this occurs, the creditor will receive at least a portion of what the firm owes. This is obviously much more favorable than losing everything if liquidation takes place. So the creditor compromises on the obligation in order to avoid a total loss. However, the TDR does not guarantee payment of debt but merely makes it easier for the debtor to meet the obligation. A TDR may result in a situation where the debtor firm still cannot satisfy its obligations. If this occurs, the firm may be forced to file for bankruptcy and possible liquidation.

It is important for a firm to be able to pinpoint trouble spots and know how to correct them. A firm that has realized that operating results are deteriorating can take steps to improve its condition. The firm must first determine why its operating results are declining. Once the cause is known, the proper actions can be taken. For example, a firm's selling price may be higher than its competition's, thus reducing the firm's sales. A proper response might be to increase advertising or reduce the selling price of the product.

When a firm does not identify its early trouble spots and take corrective measures and thus experiences deteriorating results for several years, its possible alternatives include loan default, merger, or a troubled debt restructuring. If the firm wants to continue to be an independent going concern, a TDR may be its best alternative. With the agreement of the creditors, the payment of debt can be prolonged or reduced, allowing the firm to reverse its deteriorating position. Again, it is emphasized that the creditors must consent to a TDR. It is hoped that the firm will again become profitable and settle its debts with its creditors within the TDR time frame. If this is not possible, or the creditors will not allow a restructuring, the firm may wish to merge with another firm and, therefore, continue to operate. Otherwise, loan default is imminent and this often leads to bankruptcy, and possibly liquidation.

Argenti, in his book *Corporate Collapse: The Causes and Symptoms*, discusses the topic of early identification of failure and its prevention. He presents reasons for the increase in bankruptcy, such as economic downturn and the growing size of firms in recent years. Firms that rapidly increase their growth sometimes need better managers than they can find. Good management requires experienced people with good training. When a firm needs managers, sometimes these factors are ignored. Argenti recognizes the need to develop a framework for explaining failure. If and when the causes of business failure can be determined, action can be taken to prevent those events from occurring.

Argenti quotes several authors who have written concerning the causes of failure, which include top management, accounting information, change, accounting manipulations, rapid expansion, and the economic cycle. Another chapter is devoted to the classic Altman study (1968), which is discussed later in this section.

Following an analysis of the Rolls Royce and Penn Central collapses, Argenti presents his opinions pertaining to the causes and symptoms of failure. He defines three types of failure. The first type occurs in newly formed, smaller companies, which never grow to be successful in their short lives. The second type of failure also occurs with very young firms, who grow fast in their initial years and become profitable firms. However, in the last few years of their life they literally collapse. The third type of failure occurs with long-lived, previously successful firms, whose demise takes several years of deteriorating conditions.

Argenti ends his book with ideas for the prevention and cure of failure. He includes suggestions for what government, banks, and shareholders can do to help. Although Argenti does not develop a theory of business failure, he took the initial step by analyzing the characteristics of failed firms.

Most studies in the bankruptcy area have attempted to classify firms as being either failed or non-failed from one to several years prior to business failure. The purpose of classifying failed and non-failed firms into their proper categories is to develop some type of model that can predict which firms in a group of non-bankrupt firms will experience bankruptcy in the future. The results of the classification models have been good. These models have classified over 90 percent of their given samples accurately. However, when they are used for prediction, the results have been poor.

Classification accuracy drops significantly when these models are used to analyze other samples of firms. Research in this area indicates that good classification results are roughly 90 percent or better for one year prior to bankruptcy, 80 percent or better for two years prior to bankruptcy, and 70 percent or better for three or more years prior to bankruptcy (e.g., see Altman, 1968 or Beaver, 1966).

Most studies in the area have been ex-post, classifying firms as failed or non-failed after the failed group has filed for bankruptcy. Their ex-post nature has been considered to be a weakness since these models have classified these firms well but do not predict well in an ex-ante framework. It is believed that these ex-post studies will eventually produce ex-ante studies which can predict bankruptcy with better accuracy, but the research in the bankruptcy area has not reached this point thus far.

The most common types of firms studied have been large industrial firms. Data from these firms can be more easily obtained (e.g., 10-K reports, *Moody's*

Manuals, and the COMPUSTAT Industrial Research File). Other types of firms studied have been railroads (Altman, 1973), savings and loan associations (Altman, 1977), small businesses (Edmister, 1972), banks (Sinkey, 1975), and retail firms (Altman, Haldeman, and Narayanan, 1977).

Financial ratios have been the most commonly used variables in the classification models. However, other variables such as price-level statements (Norton and Smith, 1979; Mensah, 1983) and market price data (Beaver, 1973) have also been studied. The hypothesis is that various financial ratios will be significantly different for failed versus non-failed firms. The basic categories of ratios studied have been based on liquidity, profitability, coverage, and other earnings, relative to leverage measures, capitalization, and earnings variability (Rose and Giroux, 1980). Various studies have found different specific ratios to be the most significant, but there has been overlapping since different studies have used some of the same ratios.

The methodologies employed have also varied. Univariate methods have been used, which consider the effect of one variable at a time. These methods do not reflect the interactions of the variables being studied so they are considered to be inferior. Yet, using this method a significant variable for predicting bankruptcy can be pinpointed. For example, Beaver (1966) found that cash flow was an important predictor variable.

Multivariate methods do consider the interactions for the variables involved. The most widely used method up to this point has been multiple discriminant analysis (MDA) (Altman et al., 1977). One of the assumptions of MDA is that there are at least two discrete and known groups. In Altman's study there are two discrete groups: bankrupt and nonbankrupt firms; each bankrupt firm is matched with a nonbankrupt firm. Although matching is not required, it has been done in the finance literature in an attempt to assure similarity between samples in all characteristics except bankrupt-nonbankrupt (Rose and Giroux, 1980). In Altman's study, the samples were matched by firm size, type of firm, and other factors so that every two firms matched together were as similar as possible, with the exception of their bankruptcy status.

MDA selects the best variables for classification and combines them into a predictive model. Then it classifies observations into either bankrupt or nonbankrupt categories using the individual firms' predictive ratios.

Other multivariate methods which have been used are linear regression and LOGIT (Ohlson, 1980). These methods have not performed as well as MDA, so they will not be discussed here. They have resulted in good classification accuracy, but not as good as MDA. Neither achieved 90 percent accuracy one year prior to bankruptcy.

Beaver (1966, 1968, 1973) was one of the first to attempt to classify firms into failed and non-failed categories. He defined failure as the inability to pay obligations as they matured. He used 79 pairs of large industrial firms. Data were obtained from *Moody's Manuals*. He compared financial ratios and market prices as predictors using univariate techniques and found that two ratios, cash flow/total debt and net income/total assets, were the most successful in classifying firms up to three years prior to failure.

Wilcox (1971) developed a theoretical model to explain Beaver's results, since there had been no theory of bankruptcy to date. He developed a model to determine the probability of ultimate failure and found that the components of his model were similar to Beaver's best ratios (cash flow). He suggests that additional research into the variance of cash inflows, cash outflows, and the covariance of cash inflows and outflows may result in a better predictive bankruptcy model.

Wilcox's theoretical model did not go without criticism. Benishay (1973) found it unappealing and unrealistic. The theoretical model, he said, is not a predictive model, but an "autopsy analysis" of failed firms. Again, this is a common criticism of all the empirical studies to date. Kinney (1973) noted that Beaver's 1966 model produced comparable results using fewer data and less computation. However, Wilcox's attempt at a theoretical model to explain bankruptcy may have been a necessary step to the bankruptcy theory which is so badly needed.

In a later study, Wilcox (1973) developed a cash flow model to predict bankruptcy. His study tests his previously developed statistic derived from the binomial expansion. This model classified well up to five years prior to bankruptcy.

Deakin (1972) used the 14 ratios employed in Beaver's study along with MDA to determine if MDA would give Beaver's model better predictive accuracy. The ratios were as follows: cash flow/total debt, net income/total assets, total debt/total assets, current assets/total assets, quick assets/total assets, working capital/total assets, cash/total assets, current assets/current liabilities, quick assets/current liabilities, cash/current liabilities, current assets/sales, quick assets/sales, working capital/sales, and cash/sales. The failed firms in Deakin's study were companies which experienced bankruptcy, insolvency, or liquidation. The failed firms tended to expand through debt and preferred stock in the third and fourth years prior to failure. The MDA model had very good results for up to three years prior to bankruptcy. When Deakin applied the model to an independent sample, the second and third year prior to failure had good results but not the first year prior to failure. Deakin could not explain this result.

Altman (1968) used 66 manufacturing companies to assess the quality of ratio analysis. This was a landmark study in the bankruptcy literature. The failed firm group comprised legally bankrupt firms under Chapter X or Chapter XI of the National Bankruptcy Act. He used MDA to test his five best ratios: working capital/total assets, retained earnings/total assets, earnings before interest and taxes/total assets, market value of equity/book value of debt, and sales/total assets.

Altman was the first to employ MDA for the classification of failed and nonfailed firms. The model had a classification accuracy of 94 percent for one year prior to bankruptcy and 72 percent for two years prior to bankruptcy (Altman, 1968). Since Altman, using MDA, had better results than previous researchers (e.g., Beaver), several studies thereafter have used MDA. Different variables have been analyzed in an attempt to improve classification accuracy.

Moyer (1977) tested a new sample of firms using Altman's classic model and got very poor results. He then re-estimated Altman's parameters using stepwise MDA and found the model got better classification accuracy by omitting two of the five variables. Those variables were market value of equity/book value of debt and sales/total assets. Two possible explanations were offered:

1. The significance of the variables is sensitive to the sample data examined.
2. Discriminant analysis is not valid to test the significance of the variables, as asserted earlier by Joy and Tollefson.

Moyer also found that, when compared to Beaver's model, the Altman model stands up well. So again, MDA proved to be more accurate than previously used univariate methods.

Altman, Haldeman, and Narayanan (1977) constructed a new bankruptcy classification model called ZETA. ZETA classifies very accurately up to five years prior to bankruptcy. In addition to manufacturing firms, the sample in this study also contained retail firms. The authors cite several reasons for developing a new model despite the accuracy of the older models:

1. The change in size, and financial profile, of business failures in re-cent years warranted new research.
2. The data being used are from a newer time period (1970s).
3. Retail firms are included.
4. The data and footnotes have been analyzed to include most recent changes in financial reporting standards and accepted accounting practices.
5. Several advances and controversial aspects of MDA not previously addressed were tested here.

A seven-variable model was developed and tested using both linear and quadratic MDA. These variables dealt with return on assets, stability of earnings, debt service, cumulative profitability, liquidity, capitalization, and size. If the variance-covariance matrices of the two groups of failed and non-failed firms had been identical, linear MDA would be appropriate. If not, quadratic MDA should be used; it was determined that quadratic MDA was appropriate for testing the model. However, when linear MDA was used, bankruptcy classification was more accurate.

The ZETA model was compared with Altman's 1968 model in three ways. First the older model was tested for five years. This resulted in poor prediction accuracy after the second year. Second, the sample from the ZETA model was used in Altman's model. Finally, new parameters were calculated for the new sample based on the variables in the Altman model. The ZETA model proved superior in each comparison.

Finally, the efficiency of the ZETA model was tested by comparing it to two naive strategies where all firms were classified as nonbankrupt and a proportional chance strategy was based on observed error rates equalling a prior probability. ZETA was found to be almost six times as efficient as the two naive strategies.

Rose and Giroux (1980), in a later study, used MDA to develop their own bankruptcy classification model. In this study, firms were used which had filed petitions under Chapter X or Chapter XI of the National Bankruptcy Act between 1970 and 1978. The data were obtained from the COMPUSTAT Industrial Research File, the largest data base available. The authors tested 130 variables for their predictive significance. A quadratic MDA model was then developed using the best 18 predictive ratios. Some of the ratios examined here were pre-tax profit margin, current assets/total assets, operating profit margin after depreciation, and the current ratio. This model resulted in good classification accuracy up to seven years prior to bankruptcy.

Rose and Giroux suggest that, with further research, an "early warning system" can be developed to find trouble spots for companies which could help them avoid failure. In their sample, the failed firms experienced similar problems:

1. An expense problem, especially selling, general, and administrative
2. A smaller cash flow margin
3. More rapid turnover of receivables and inventories
4. Lower earnings
5. High financial leverage
6. Low liquidity
7. Reduced dividend yields

Rose and Giroux found that linear MDA was more successful when classifying firms as failed or non-failed than quadratic MDA but was also more erratic over time. The success of their model over previous studies is due to the use of the COMPUSTAT Industrial File and the MULDIS MDA package, an efficient approach to utilizing the COMPUSTAT data.

Several other studies have been conducted which give similar results. Blum's failing company model (1974) was developed to predict failure for 115 pairs of industrial firms. His variables incorporate changes over time which other models do not. Some of his variables are net quick assets/inventory, cash flow/total liabilities, standard deviation of net income over a period, and net worth at book value/total liabilities. Firms were considered failed when they were unable to pay debts as they came due, entered into bankruptcy proceedings, or entered into debt restructuring to reduce debt with creditors. He used financial ratios and discriminant analysis and achieved classification accuracy up to five years prior to failure.

Dambolena and Khoury (1980) used financial ratios and MDA to classify failed and non-failed firms. They noted that ratios for failed firms become more unstable than for non-failed firms as the firms approach bankruptcy, so their analysis included the stability of the ratios. Their model was accurate for up to five years prior to bankruptcy. The ratios they used were as follows: net profit/sales, net profit/net worth, net profit/net working capital, net profit/fixed assets, net profit/total assets, sales/net worth, sales/net working capital, sales/inventory, cost of sales/inventory, current ratio, acid test ratio, inventory/net working capital, current debt/inventory, fixed assets/net worth, current debt/net worth, total debt/net worth, times interest earned, funded debt/net working capital, and total debt/total assets.

Collins (1980) compares two Altman studies (1968, 1977) with one done by Meyer and Pifer for banks (1970). Meyer and Pifer regressed each of their financial ratios on time and determined the time trend, coefficient of variation, and shift away from the trend in the period prior to failure. Collins found that the Altman methodology classified just as well as the Meyer and Pifer methodology.

Norton and Smith (1979) used industrial firms to compare historical cost ratios with general price-level adjusted ratios. They found no significant differences in the classification accuracy between historical cost ratios and general price-level adjusted ratios.

In the most current bankruptcy study to date, Mensah (1983) developed a discriminant model similar to those developed in the past. He used the same financial ratios which had been used before, but applied price-level techniques to these variables. He also implemented LOGIT analysis. His results were insignificant, as neither of his models achieved better classification accuracy than previous ones. This would indicate that price-level changes have no effect on bankruptcy prediction.

Ohlson (1980) performed a study using financial ratios to predict bankruptcy using LOGIT. He gathered data from 10-K reports in order to obtain the data at the time they were released to the public, because he considered the timing of when information is made available to be very important. He also considered it difficult to extract data from *Moody's Manuals* because it is very condensed. He found four significant factors affecting the probability of failure within one year:

1. Company size
2. Measure(s) of financial structure
3. Measure(s) of performance
4. Measure(s) of current liquidity

The ratios employed dealt with these factors. For example, to measure size, Ohlson used the log (total assets/GNP price-level index). Net income/total assets was used as a measure of performance. Working capital/total assets was used as a liquidity measure. Total liabilities/total assets was used to measure financial structure. He chose not to use MDA because of some of the problems associated with it:

1. There are certain statistical requirements imposed on the distributional properties of the predictors (e.g., the variance-covariance matrices should be identical for the failed and non-failed groups). A normal distribution is required.
2. The output of an MDA model is a score in which the observation is classified based on an ordinal ranking device, leaving little intuitive interpretation.
3. The matching of failed and non-failed firms is somewhat arbitrary.

Ohlson's methodology, LOGIT analysis, avoids these problems. LOGIT analysis is an econometric model which determines the probability that the firm will fail within some specified time period given that it belongs to a certain population.

In Ohlson's sample, the failed firms must have filed for bankruptcy under Chapter X or Chapter XI of the National Bankruptcy Act. The non-failed firms were taken from the COMPUSTAT Industrial Research File. All firms had to be traded on some stock exchange or over-the-counter market and had to be industrial firms.

His results indicate that LOGIT analysis predicts bankruptcy accurately within one year, within two years if the company did not fail in the first year, and within one or two years. Ohlson concludes that with more research, LOGIT analysis may be a powerful predictive tool.

Scott (1981) reviews several empirical bankruptcy models derived by other researchers. From these models, he concludes that bankruptcy prediction may be possible due to low misclassification rates. He notes that earnings or cash flow and debt appear in all of the models analyzed. Another important variable in bankruptcy prediction is a firm's stock price.

Scott presents the results of the empirical models developed by Beaver (1966), Altman (1968, 1977), Ohlson (1980), and others. He notes that several ratios used in these studies are similar. Next he reviews the models based on the ''gambler's ruin'' theory. Wilcox (1971) was a pioneer with these models in which the firm is considered a gambler which is classified as nonbankrupt when its net worth is positive. When the firm's net worth drops to zero, the firm is classified as bankrupt. However, these models have not had any empirical support.

In the simple case, the firm lasts for two periods. The firm is considered bankrupt if its liabilities exceed its liquidation value. These models, then, are different from the empirical models so they cannot explain the successful results of those models. Based on Wilcox's theoretical model, Scott transforms Wilcox's 1971 gambler's ruin model and Altman's 1977 model so they contain the same stock and flow variables. Although Altman's ZETA model contains more variables, the stock and flow variables are explained theoretically.

Next, Scott develops a theoretical model based on the value of the firm and the debt it owes its creditors. His model incorporates firms which have imperfect access to capital. As measures of financial failure, he uses debt, income, retained earnings, and market value and book value of equity. He concludes that there is an overlap between the empirical and theoretical models since there are many similarities between them. Scott ends by discussing the similarities and dissimilarities between the empirical and theoretical models, and concludes that the theoretical models are too simple and have not been developed enough thus far to explain the empirical models. As these models become more sophisticated in the future, it may be possible to predict TDRs in this process. Also, these models may be able to detect which types of firms should implement TDRs.

Hamer, in an unpublished working paper derived from her dissertation (1982), compares the Altman (1968), Deakin (1972), and Blum (1974) studies with a new model she developed. Her results were similar to each of the individual studies' results. Up to five years prior to bankruptcy, prediction accuracy was good. Beyond five years prior to bankruptcy classification, accuracy was below 70 percent in all models.

In her discriminant model, she found linear MDA to classify better than quadratic MDA. She also notes that other methods that relax the assumptions of a normal distribution, particularly LOGIT, have not resulted in better classification accuracy. This result is also substantiated by Ohlson (1980), which supports the continued use of MDA in this type of study.

Hamer's study is relevant to this research for several reasons. Bankruptcy is defined in both cases as filing a petition under the National Bankruptcy Act. She uses MDA, which this study does also. She uses the MULDIS package, which is used here. Finally, both models use the COMPUSTAT files for data gathering. All of these similarities should result in similar results pertaining to the bankruptcy prediction model developed for the bankrupt and nonbankrupt firms.

Most of the empirical bankruptcy studies have agreed that financial ratios and other variables analyzed have predictive ability. Because these studies have analyzed different variables and ratios, they disagree somewhat on which ratios are the best predictors and in their percent of classification accuracy and the length of time for which each model is accurate. However, there is a great deal of overlap among these studies. For example, they agree that liquidity ratios are important, although one study may use cash flows (e.g., Beaver, 1968) and another may consider working capital more significant (e.g., Altman, 1968). Altman (1977) had good classification results for up to five years while Beaver's 1968 model classified well for only two years. The later models have achieved better classification results. All these studies have used ratios pertaining to liquidity, profitability, coverage, and other earnings relative to leverage measures, capitalization, and earnings variability (Rose and Giroux, 1980).

Most of the variations in the previously published studies have been mentioned, but a brief list is provided here as a summary:

1. Variations in time period covered by the data (up to 10 years)
2. Variations in size of companies
3. Variations in ratios used
4. Variations in methodologies employed
5. Variations in the industries used
6. Variations in the definition of failure

These variations are responsible for the differences between the bankruptcy models. In general, though, it is agreed that failure can be predicted from events occurring several years prior to failure. There is also agreement about which types of ratios are the best predictors; these studies support the failure process theory which is an underlying assumption of this study.

3

Methodology

In this chapter, a description of the methodology employed in this study will be presented. First, selection procedures for the three samples used are discussed. Next, the statistical design used is discussed in detail. Variable selection procedures and validation testing are presented. Finally, the hypotheses to be tested in order to analyze the TDR firms are presented.

Sample Selection

It was first necessary to draw three samples for this study. In order to develop a bankruptcy model using MDA, a sample of industrial bankrupt firms filing petitions under Chapter X or Chapter XI of the National Bankruptcy Act was found. Under the National Bankruptcy Act, creditors may file an Involuntary Petition in Bankruptcy or debtors may file a voluntary petition under Chapter XI of the Bankruptcy Code. Here, the debtor firm attempts to work out an agreement with its creditors so it may become a going concern again and hence avoid liquidation. The Bankruptcy Tax Act of 1980 provides for several tax advantages for the bankrupt firm, including a new type of reorganization qualifying for tax-free treatment.

The *Wall Street Journal Index* is the source from which the bankrupt firms were chosen. Each of these firms was cross-referenced through *Moody's Investor Manuals* and SEC 10-K reports to determine its specific filing dates for bankruptcy. The bankrupt firms were selected from a 10-year period, 1972–81, since variables which predict bankruptcy may change over time. Rose and Giroux (1980), for example, used a 10-year time period. A time period of this length makes it possible to obtain a good sample size from the COMPUSTAT Industrial File. Altman (1968) used a 20-year time period. In choosing a time period for analysis, the economic cycles must be taken into consideration. The 10-year period from 1972 to 1981 was a period of both inflation and recession in which business failures increased; for these reasons, this time period was chosen for analysis.

When using MDA, large samples increase predictive ability (Eisenbeis and Avery, 1972). Previous studies (Altman, 1968; Rose and Giroux, 1980) have used sample sizes of between 30 and 35. Therefore, a sample size of at least 30 should be appropriate here (Tatsuoka, 1971). Large samples increase the likelihood that the hypothesis of the equality of group means and dispersions will be rejected (Eisenbeis and Avery, 1972). Using a normal multivariate technique, a sample size of around 25 is considered adequate. Another factor which will influence the sample size is the MULDIS package being used. In order for MULDIS to compute a discriminant function, the number of variables tested must be less than the sample size used. In this study, 25 variables were tested, which means that the sample size must be significantly greater than 25. Since the sample size was only 35, the 12 variables selected by MULDIS were retested by themselves. MULDIS selected all 12 of these variables for the discriminant function.

The COMPUSTAT Industrial Research File was examined to determine how many of these 35 firms it included. This file provides a large data base from which the model could be developed. Firms listed on the COMPUSTAT Industrial File are all publicly traded companies. It has been used in past studies because of the vast amount of data it contains. Only failed firms appearing on the COMPUSTAT Industrial Research Tape were used for analysis. Therefore, all the bankrupt firms used in the analysis are publicly traded firms. See appendix A for a list of these firms and the year each one filed for bankruptcy.

Next, a sample of industrial nonbankrupt firms was chosen from the COMPUSTAT Industrial File. These firms were matched with the bankrupt firms by type and size. When using MDA, two or more discrete groups are needed for analysis; in this case, the two groups are the bankrupt and nonbankrupt firms. Since the prediction of bankruptcy is desired, the two groups were matched so that they were as similar as possible with the exception of their bankrupt or nonbankrupt status. The samples include both industrial and retail firms.

As part of the matching process, each nonbankrupt firm is in the same industry as its bankrupt counterpart. In other words, the Standard and Poor's industry code is the same for each matched pair. Also, total assets and sales for matched firms do not differ by more than 10 percent, because differences greater than 10 percent are generally considered significant (Tatsuoka, 1971).

Finally, a sample of debt-restructured firms was obtained from DISCLOSURE, Inc. No known index exists which provides a complete listing of debt-restructured firms, but DISCLOSURE, Inc., a computerized service, provides a listing of all publicly traded debt-restructured firms. Firms can be selected according to the specific disclosures made in their financial statements. Approximately 9,000 firms comprise the DISCLOSURE population; these firms are listed on the New York Stock Exchange, American Stock Exchange, and Over-the-Counter Exchange. In this particular study, firms were selected from a total of 76 which made disclosure of debt restructuring in one year. This is the most complete sample available of TDR firms. The sample was used in the analysis after eliminating those firms which either had not, in fact, restructured their debt or were actually creditors, not debtors, of a TDR, i.e., banks, bank holding companies, and real estate companies. Again, each of these firms was cross-referenced with Moody's investor service manuals and SEC 10-K reports to determine the specific dates of debt restructuring.

The sample of TDR firms consists of both industrial and retail firms. This is consistent with the bankrupt and nonbankrupt samples. Several of the TDR firms have the same SIC industry code as some of the bankrupt and nonbankrupt firms.

The size of the TDR firms in relation to the bankrupt and nonbankrupt firms is also an important factor. The bankrupt and nonbankrupt firms are all large firms with assets over one million dollars, since they are all listed on the COMPUSTAT Industrial File. Therefore, the TDR firms also should be large firms so that they can be more comparable with the bankrupt and nonbankrupt firms.

The mean asset size of the bankrupt firms was $122.32 million and the mean asset size of the nonbankrupt firms was $109.88 million. Both samples had large variances since assets ranged from $1.2 million to well over one billion dollars. The TDR sample had a mean asset size of $285.98 million, which is substantially larger than the other samples; however, all but three of the firms fell in the same range as the bankrupt and nonbankrupt samples. Two had assets under one million dollars while one had assets over two billion dollars. Therefore, the size of the TDR firms is fairly comparable to the bankrupt and nonbankrupt samples. When these three firms were not included, the mean asset size of the TDR firms was $119.41 million, i.e., the majority of firms in the TDR sample had a mean asset size between the bankrupt and nonbankrupt firms. The variances for all three samples were extremely large.

Of the 76 firms selected for analysis, it was found that eight actually did not enter into a TDR nor did they intend to do so, and these were eliminated from further analysis. This may indicate that the DISCLOSURE data base is not totally reliable; however, it is the only data base currently available, so it had to be used in this study. Another eight firms were banks, bank holding companies, and real estate companies and were also dropped from the sample. As a result, a total of 60 TDR firms were left for analysis. For a breakdown of the TDR sample, see table 1.

Selected variables were chosen from the bankrupt sample for one, two, and three years prior to bankruptcy. Classification accuracy beyond three years prior to bankruptcy may not be reliable (Altman, 1968); the results of the various studies have been mixed. The same variables are chosen for the matched nonbankrupt firms for the same years as their bankrupt counterparts. Finally, the selected variables are chosen for the TDR sample for one, two, and three years prior to bankruptcy.

The three samples of firms are mutually exclusive, so that there is no inter-action of data between firms. The bankrupt sample is composed of 35 firms which filed for bankruptcy in the period 1972–81 and were listed on the COMPUSTAT Industrial File. The matched nonbankrupt sample also contains 35 firms. Finally, the TDR sample contains 60 firms. For a list of the firms in the three samples, see appendix A.

Table 1

Compilation of TDR Sample

Number of firms selected by DISCLOSURE, Inc.   76

Less:

    Number of firms with no TDR   8

    Banks   6

    Bank Holding Companies   1

    Real Estate Companies   1
                                                              16

Debtor TDR firms Left for Analysis   60

The reason for using three samples is first to compute a bankruptcy prediction model. In order to determine if the TDR sample follows the failure process, these firms are analyzed with the bankruptcy model. In this manner, it can be seen whether the TDR firms become more like the bankrupt firms prior to TDR. If the bankruptcy continuum holds, this result should occur.

Statistical Design

Using multiple discriminant analysis (MDA), a prediction model was developed similar to the Rose and Giroux model (1980). Discriminant analysis is a multivariate statistical technique which classifies observations into two or more qualitative categories by using two or more quantitative variables. The following assumptions are necessary in order for discriminant analysis to be valid (Eisenbeis and Avery, 1972):

1)   there are two or more discrete and known groups
2)   each observation in each group has a set of at least two characteristics (variables) and,
3)   the groups (populations) have multivariate normal distributions with common covariance matrices.

The purposes of discriminant analysis are as follows (Eisenbeis and Avery, 1972):

1)   to test for mean group differences and to describe the overlaps among groups and
2)   to construct classification schemes based upon the set of m variables in order to assign previously unclassified observations to the appropriate groups.

The techniques used in discriminant analysis are multivariate extensions of univariate analysis of variance. In the application of discriminant analysis, the goal is to assign the observations to the most similar groups while trying to minimize misclassifications.

Discriminant analysis determines the direction of group differences by finding a linear combination of the original predictor variables that shows large differences in group means. First, a criterion must be chosen to measure group-mean differences. The F-ratio is used for testing the significance of the overall difference among several group means on a single variable. The F-ratio is computed as follows:

$$F = \frac{SSb \ / \ N-K}{SSw \ / \ K-1}$$

where K is the number of groups, N is the number of observations, SSb is the between sum-of squares, and SSw is the within sum-of squares.

The linear discriminant function can then be written as follows:

$$Z = v1 \ X \ 1 + v2 \ X \ 2 + \ldots + vp \ X \ p$$

Here there are p predictor variables denoted as X. In this equation, Z is the computed discriminant score and the v's are the coefficients or weights for the predictor variables.

The optimal discriminant function occurs when SSb is maximized. At that point, the coefficients are determined. Matrices and vectors can be used when the number of coefficients needed becomes large.

In discriminant analysis, the equation using the number of variables which best discriminate between two or more groups is selected. The number of discriminant variables necessary to describe all between-group variation is the minimum of the between-group degrees of freedom and the number of variates.

There are three hypothesis tests used in discriminant analysis. The first tests for the usefulness of the entire discriminant function. The second test determines whether a hypothetical discriminant function is in agreement with the discriminant function computed from the data. Finally, the third test determines whether a given variable should be included or excluded from the function.

In this study, the variables used for analysis are financial ratios. These have been used in prior studies and are considered to have good classification accuracy (Altman, 1968, 1977).

The development of the discriminant function entails several statistical computations. Because this becomes very complex, computers are necessary in the construction of the discriminant function. Today, there are several software packages available to do this.

In a two-group case, which is used here, these multivariate tests can be reduced to a univariate test by creating a linear function of the observation vectors. The vector B is used to transform the variable y so that the ratio of the between-groups variance of y is at a maximum (Eisenbeis and Avery, 1972).

A good classification procedure minimizes the probability of misclassification. Eisenbeis and Avery (1972) give the following function to be minimized:

$$M = P(1 \mid 2) \, \Pi_2 \, 2 + P(2 \mid 1) \, \Pi_1$$

where $P(g \mid h)$ is the probability of assigning an observation to group g, given that it arose from group h. In this case, h is the a priori probability of an observation being drawn from group h.

The function M above is then minimized as follows:

Assign to group 1 if

$$\frac{f1\ (x)}{f2\ (x)} \geq \frac{\Pi_2}{\Pi_1}$$

Assign to group 2 otherwise (Eisenbeis and Avery, 1972). An observation that is incorrectly assigned to group 1 is called a Type I error, and an observation that is incorrectly assigned to group 2 is called a Type II error.

The computer package MULDIS is used to develop a bankruptcy prediction model by selecting the financial ratios from the firms which are most significant in predicting bankruptcy. MDA is used to take a given set of variables, in this case the financial ratios, and compute the linear and/or quadratic equation from them which best discriminates between two populations. The equation developed may use from one up to all of the variables tested. Each variable selected in the equation will have a coefficient assigned to it. This equation has the fewest classification errors.

Linear classification may be used when the population dispersions are equal, but when they are unequal, quadratic classification procedures should be used (Eisenbeis and Avery, 1972). In previous studies, however, linear classification actually performed better than quadratic even when the population dispersions were unequal (Rose and Giroux, 1980; McCall and Eisenbeis, 1970). MULDIS determined that the variance-covariance matrices were not equal. Also, MULDIS computes both linear and quadratic discriminant functions. It was found that the linear model had better classification accuracy, and therefore it was used in this study. As mentioned in chapter 1, linear MDA has been shown to be powerful even when the assumption of equal population dispersions is violated.·

Each firm is assigned a Z score based on its own financial ratios and the discriminant function. A critical value (Zc) is also determined, so that any Z values above Zc are classified as nonbankrupt and any Z values below Zc are classified as bankrupt.

The MULDIS package chosen for this study is considered to be one of the best packages available and has been used for over ten years (Rose and Giroux, 1980). It has been successfully implemented in previous bankruptcy studies (see Rose and Giroux, 1980, or Hamer, 1982). It has many statistical options available. They are as follows (Eisenbeis and Avery, 1972):

1. the calculation of discriminant functions and related significance tests;
2. the use of classification rules to assign new observations to the appropriate groups;
3. the calculation of discriminant functions and related tests and reduced space means and dispersions matrices;
4. the calculation of discriminant functions and related tests, and the use of classification rules to assign new observations to the appropriate groups (test space classification only);
5. the calculation of the discriminant functions and related tests, the calculation of reduced space means and dispersion matrices, and the use of classification rules to assign new observations to the appropriate groups.

In addition, a wide range of secondary options is available, including:

1. the Box test of group dispersion equality;
2. complete, forward, and backward stepwise selection procedures;
3. test space or reduced space linear or quadratic classification procedures;
4. the Lachenbruch holdout classification method;
5. printouts of the actual classification equations and rules;
6. graphs of the original and classified observations in linear reduced space;
7. various print, labeling, and punched output.

The Lachenbruch holdout classification method was used in this study (see following section). When this method is used, the graph option listed above cannot be used. However, of main importance here are the calculation of discriminant functions, forward and backward stepwise procedures, and the Lachenbruch holdout classification method.

Selection of Variables

The two dependent variables of interest here are failed and non-failed. The independent variables consist of selected financial ratios. Those ratios chosen best classified the bankrupt-nonbankrupt status of each firm through the MDA function. The ratios analyzed were those most commonly employed in earlier studies. The discriminant function attempts to maximize classification accuracy in the selection of these ratios.

The financial ratios chosen for analysis came from the Altman studies (1968, 1977). As of 1980, these models were recognized as being the most accurate in the literature (Dambolena and Khoury, 1980). (See appendix B for the specific ratios analyzed.) The ratios found to have significant discriminating power were used to develop the discriminant function. Forward stepwise procedures eliminate those ratios which do not have significant predictive ability. These ratios are also listed in appendix B.

Over the past several years, hundreds of ratios have been tested for their classification accuracy. Altman was a pioneer in implementing MDA. His models have had good classification accuracy in comparison to other models. Classification results are considered to be good when there is 90 percent correct classification accuracy for one year prior to bankruptcy (Rose and Giroux, 1980). Therefore, the financial statement items used in his study were used here to compute 25 ratios from these data. The F-statistic calculated for the 12-variable set selected from this set of 25 was 14.64867, which is significant at a level of .0001. The percent of classification accuracy of each variable is shown in appendix B. Next, stepwise forward selection MDA is used to select those variables with the greatest discriminating power. The MULDIS package performs this function. The stepwise procedures perform discriminant functions on different sets of variables. One variable is eliminated at a time. The set of variables which best classifies the discrete samples is then selected. The best set of variables is determined when Wilks' lambda is minimized. Wilks' lambda is an inverse measure of the discriminating power of the ratios (Eisenbeis and Avery, 1972).

Validation Testing

Validation testing of the discriminant function is necessary, since the specific model employed may only accurately classify firms for the sample of firms for which it was developed. When testing the classification accuracy for the function, the same sample of firms tested will produce the minimum classification errors, since this was the sample from which the function was developed. In other words, the MDA model is sample specific. Another sample of firms with different ratios may not achieve the same classification success. This should not be the case, since the function should discriminate accurately for any given sample within the same underlying population. Therefore, the model should not be validated using the original sample (Joy and Tollefson, 1975).

A common technique for validation testing used in earlier studies was to split the firms into two groups. The model was developed on one group, while the other group was used for validation. Altman used this procedure in his original classic study (1968). Scott (1979) criticized the use of a holdout sample where samples are small, because this technique can lead to poor estimates and incorrect conclusions about the error rates of the discriminant functions.

Another validation technique, developed by Lachenbruch (1975), results in an almost unbiased estimate of error rates for all sample observations. It is an iterative technique where each observation is held out from the sample. The Lachenbruch method combines the features of using the original sample and holdout sample for validation testing. After each observation is held out from the sample, it is then reclassified. The proportion of misclassified observations is then used to determine the classification accuracy of the discriminant function. The discriminant function is then estimated using all remaining observations. Scott (1979) concludes that this technique of validation is clearly superior.

Rose and Giroux (1980) implemented the Lachenbruch technique in their study. They achieved results superior to previous bankruptcy studies in that their model accurately classified firms as failed and non-failed up to seven years prior to bankruptcy. The best previous model (Altman, 1977) accurately classified firms up to five years prior to bankruptcy. The Lachenbruch technique for validation testing is employed in this study, both because of its accuracy and because the samples involved are relatively small. The MULDIS computer package used here includes the Lachenbruch validation technique.

The model is developed using the sample of paired bankrupt and nonbankrupt firms. Any firms classified as nonbankrupt which are actually bankrupt are considered a Type I error. Any firms classified as bankrupt which are actually nonbankrupt are considered a Type II error. The results can be condensed as illustrated in table 2. From these results, the percent classified correctly can be easily obtained. This is important to ensure good classification accuracy. A model without good classification accuracy cannot be expected to predict or classify well when applied to other firms.

After the model has been developed and tested for its accuracy, the TDR firms are tested. The TDR firms are tested for one, two, and three years prior to restructuring to determine if they classify as failed or non-failed. If the TDR firms are heading toward bankruptcy, then prior to TDR, a larger percent of these firms may classify as bankrupt. This result would be expected if the failure process holds. However, it may be too soon for these firms to classify as bankrupt. If the failure process does not hold, or if TDR is not part of this process, then the TDR firms may not classify as bankrupt before debt restructuring. If not, they may continue to fall in the failed category.

A Z score distribution is developed for the TDR sample as well as for the bankrupt and nonbankrupt samples. In this manner it can be determined if the Z score distribution for the TDR sample approximates either the bankrupt or nonbankrupt samples, or if it has a unique distribution.

For those firms which restructured their debt more than one year before this study, further analysis is done to determine the effects of the TDR. In other words,

Table 2
MDA Results Table

Actual	Predicted	Bankrupt	Nonbankrupt
Bankrupt		H	M_1
Nonbankrupt		M_2	H

H - correct classifications (HITS)

M_1 - Type I error

M_2 - Type II error

Source: Adapted from Altman, 1968

if the TDR has helped the firms, they should change their status from failed to non-failed after the TDR.

Comparison of TDR Firms

The sample of TDR firms selected for analysis is examined for the presence or absence of several characteristics. An effort is made to determine if any similarities, such as industry type, firm size, or specific financial ratios, exist within the population of TDR firms. Specific characteristics pertaining to TDR firms have never been clearly defined, so this information could be useful to firms as an "early warning" system of financial difficulty.

The TDR firms are analyzed for several years prior to TDR. Trends within each firm are determined (e.g., increasing debt, poor operating results). Trends which differentiate these TDR firms from other firms are also analyzed. This analysis is descriptive in nature.

Hypotheses to Be Tested

In order to test for changes in Z scores from year to year, the TDR firms are tested for differences in each of their Z scores from three years prior to TDR through three years after TDR. Therefore, if Z scores are getting either better or worse from year to year for a particular firm, this change can be pinpointed.

The following hypotheses are tested:

(One-sided)

H0:   The difference in mean Z scores before TDR from one year to the next for the TDR firms is less than or equal to zero.

H1:   The difference in mean Z scores before TDR from one year to the next for the TDR firms is greater than zero.

(Two-sided)

H0:   The difference in mean Z scores after TDR from one year to the next for the TDR firms is zero.

H1:   The difference in mean Z scores after TDR from one year to the next for the TDR firms is not zero.

In the first hypothesis, if the differences in Z scores are greater than zero, Z scores are getting worse as the firms approach the TDR date. Likewise, in the second hypothesis, if the differences in Z scores are not equal to zero, then the Z scores are either getting better or worse as the firms approach TDR. If the differences in Z scores are greater than zero, the firms are getting worse, since the Z scores are declining. Conversely, if the differences in Z scores are less than zero, the firms are becoming stronger, as the values of Z scores are increasing.

The hypotheses are tested using data for a one-year period for each comparison. First, the two samples contain the Z scores for three and two years prior to TDR. Next, Z scores for two and one years prior to TDR are compared followed by one year prior to TDR and year of TDR. Z scores are also tested for the year of TDR and one year after TDR, one year after TDR and two years after TDR, and finally for two and three years after TDR.

Rejection of the first null hypothesis leads to the conclusion that Z scores of the TDR firms are getting worse as time progresses, indicating weakening firms. Rejection of the second null hypothesis leads to the conclusion that the Z scores are getting better as time progresses, indicating strengthening firms. So the financial condition of the TDR sample can be followed for several years.

In order to carry out this test, a non-parametric statistical technique is used. It is unclear whether or not normality will be found in the Z score distributions. Therefore, non-parametric tests are used, since they are robust enough to use even when normality does not exist. As previously mentioned in the limitations sections, MDA assumes multivariate normality. However, MDA has been found to be a powerful test, even when this requirement is violated. Eisenbeis and Avery

(1972) cite several studies where this has occurred. Also, to date there is no non-parametric counterpart for MDA. So, for the discriminant function, the only tool available is a parametric test.

The Wilcoxin matched-pairs, signed-ranks test is used to test for these population differences. This test uses two related samples when the relative magnitudes of differences are known. The differences are then ranked, and these rankings are used to test for differences between the related samples. In this study, two years of data are used for the same sample so that any progression toward or away from bankruptcy can be noticed.

The assumptions of the Wilcoxin matched-pairs, signed-ranks test are as follows (Daniel, 1978):

A. The data for analysis consist of n values of the difference $D_i = Y_i - X_i$. Each pair of measurements (X_i, Y_i) is taken on the same subject or on subjects that have been paired with respect to one or more variables. The sample of (X_i, Y_i) pairs is random.
B. The differences represent observations on a continuous random variable.
C. The distribution of the population of differences is symmetric.
D. The differences are independent.
E. The differences are measured on at least an interval scale.

This test, therefore, will indicate if in fact Z scores for the TDR sample worsen before the TDR date. Also, the test will indicate if Z scores for these firms get better after TDR and it will measure significant changes in Z scores before and after TDR (see table 3). In a situation where a bimodal distribution exists, the Wilcoxin matched-pairs, signed-ranks test still tests for differences in Z scores for each TDR firm.

Table 3
Frequency Table

<u>2nd Year Z Scores</u>

		Bankrupt	Nonbankrupt	Total
1st year	Bankrupt	A	B	A&B
Z scores	Nonbankrupt	C	D	C&D
Total		A&C	B&D	N

If TDR has helped firms to avoid bankruptcy and become profitable concerns again, then, after restructuring, a significantly larger number of firms should be classified as nonbankrupt. Some firms may become bankrupt after debt restructuring; therefore, these firms should be classified as bankrupt. Finally, since it may take a long period of time for a firm to turn itself around, it is possible for more and more of the TDR firms to become classified as nonbankrupt further into the future (e.g., year 3 after TDR may contain more nonbankrupt TDR firms than year 1 after TDR).

Next, the TDR sample is tested using frequencies. Again using two years of data at a time for analysis, a frequency table can be set up as shown in table 3.

The null hypothesis to be tested here is as follows: The proportion of TDR firms being classified as bankrupt is the same under two years. We let p1 be the proportion of TDR firms classified as bankrupt in one year, and p2, the proportion of TDR firms classified as bankrupt in the next year. We may state the null and alternative hypotheses symbolically as follows:

$$H0: \quad p1 = p2 \text{ or } p1 - p2 = 0$$
$$H1: \quad p1 \neq p2 \text{ or } p1 - p2 \neq 0 \text{ (Daniel, 1978)}.$$

In this manner, the frequency of firms changing their bankruptcy status from year to year can be analyzed. For years prior to TDR, if firms are weakening, there will be more firms falling into box C. After TDR, if firms are beginning to turn around, there should be more firms falling into box B.

To test for these frequencies, the McNemar test for related samples will be used. The assumptions of the McNemar test are as follows:

1. The data consist of N subjects (or items) or pairs of subjects, depending on whether subjects act as their own controls or whether experimental subjects are paired with a matched control. The data available for analysis may be displayed in a table similar to table 3.
2. The measurement scale is nominal, with four categories. Using the notation of table 3, the four categories are bankrupt-bankrupt, bankrupt-nonbankrupt, nonbankrupt-bankrupt, and nonbankrupt-nonbankrupt.
3. When subjects are their own controls, they are independent of each other. Of course, the two observations made on the same subject are related, since they are made on the same individual. When matched pairs are used the pairs are independent, but observations within a given pair are related.

Rejection of the null hypothesis would indicate that the firms are changing with respect to their bankruptcy status from year to year. In this study this test is carried out using two years of data beginning three years prior to TDR through three years after TDR. Therefore, any changes occurring in a particular year are noticed.

To test for differences before and after restructuring within the TDR firms, the Wilcoxin signed-rank test is used. This procedure uses the magnitude of median differences in one sample when testing for differences between the observed values and the hypothesized median. This test has an efficiency of 95.5 percent of the parametric t-test. The assumptions of this test are as follows (Daniel, 1978):

1. The sample available for analysis is a random sample of size n from a population with unknown median M.
2. The variable of interest is continuous.
3. The sampled population is symmetric.
4. The scale of measurement is at least interval.
5. The observations are independent.

The hypothesis to be tested here is as follows:

$$H0: \ M = M0 \qquad H1: \ M \neq M0$$

In this test, M is the firms' mean Z scores and M0 is the hypothesized median of Z scores. This analysis should evaluate restructuring of the TDR firms without using the bankrupt firms for comparison. The results should prove similar to those obtained from the above hypotheses. If there has been a trend of increasing Z scores after TDR, the Wilcoxin signed-rank test will verify this trend. Otherwise, no significant trend in Z scores after TDR will be found.

The next hypothesis to be tested here determines if a dichotomy exists for TDR firms after TDR. It is reasonable to assume that some TDR firms will turn around and become profitable while others will go into default, and ultimately bankruptcy. A chi-square test for homogeneity is appropriate here. The hypothesis to be tested is as follows:

H0: The distribution of Z scores of TDR firms is homogeneous.
H1: The distribution of Z scores of TDR firms is not homogeneous.

Again, this test is carried out for TDR firms for one, two, and three years before and after TDR. This test determines whether the TDR firms possess similar characteristics or whether there are no similarities within the TDR sample.

The assumptions of the chi-square test for homogeneity are as follows (Daniel, 1978):

1. The samples are independent.
2. The samples are random.
3. Each subject in the population may be classified into one of two mutually exclusive categories, according to whether it has or does not have the characteristic of interest.

If TDR has helped firms avoid bankruptcy, nonhomogeneity should be observed. If the trend of Z scores has increased after TDR, it is expected that one group of TDR firms will fall into the failed category and another group into the non-failed category. This result indicates nonhomogeneity. If there has been no significant trend in Z scores, the majority of firms should fall into one group, the failed category. This result indicates a homogeneous sample. Again, the results here should be consistent with those of the prior tests.

Summary

In this study, several things are analyzed. First, MDA is used to develop a bankruptcy prediction model. Using this model, the TDR sample is analyzed in order to determine the discriminant scores of the sample firms. The TDR firms are then tested to determine if they follow any particular trends of the bankrupt or nonbankrupt firms. Finally, the TDR firms are analyzed to see if or how they change after restructuring.

The following is a list of the nonparametric tests which are employed:

Hypothesis   Test
1.   The Wilcoxin matched-pairs, signed-ranks test (one-sided) determines if the TDR firms classify as bankrupt as the TDR date approaches.
2.   The Wilcoxin matched-pairs, signed-ranks test (two-sided) determines whether the TDR firms classify as bankrupt or nonbankrupt after TDR.
3.   The McNemar test for related samples determines if the proportion of TDR firms classifying as bankrupt or nonbankrupt changes over the time period used for analysis.
4.   The Wilcoxin signed-rank test determines if the number of TDR firms with positive and negative Z scores changes significantly before and after TDR.
5.   The chi-square test for homogeneity will determine if the TDR sample is homogeneous with either the bankrupt or nonbankrupt samples before and after TDR.

4

The Nature of TDR Firms

The purpose of this chapter is to examine the nature of TDR firms in detail. Since no prior studies have specifically examined TDR firms, a descriptive analysis of these firms should be useful. After analysis of the specific characteristics of these firms, some generalizations can be made about TDR firms.

A troubled debt restructuring (TDR) may occur when a firm becomes unable to pay its debts. As previously mentioned, with the creditor's approval a TDR may take a number of different forms. For example, one firm may issue common stock in exchange for debt while another may reduce its principal, and still another firm may issue common stock and reduce its principal simultaneously. The debtor may transfer real estate or other assets to the creditor to satisfy his debt. An equity interest in the firm may be issued to the creditor in order to convert the outstanding debt into equity. Finally, a modification of the terms of the debt may be agreed to, consisting of one or any combination of the following: reduction of the stated interest rate, extension of the maturity date, reduction of the face value of the debt, or a reduction of accrued interest.

TDRs have been linked to the failure process (see figure 1, p. 13). The increase in business failures more than tripled between 1978 and 1982 (*Annual Report*, Federal Reserve Bank of New York, 1982). Giroux and Wiggins (1982) state that more bankruptcies occurred during 1980 and 1981 than during the entire post-Depression period. Because of this significant increase, bankruptcy research is important and relevant to the accounting literature. If TDRs are linked to business failures as part of the failure process, then TDR research also becomes important.

To date, no one has empirically studied TDR firms. The literature which exists consists of descriptions of *FASB Statement No. 15*. In this chapter, an overall analysis will be conducted to determine the types of TDRs used by the firms in the present sample. Specific analysis of selected financial statement items and ratios will compare the TDR firms with the bankrupt and nonbankrupt samples. Next, two firms, which took different directions after TDR, will be analyzed before and after their TDR. Their financial situations will be compared prior to TDR and again after TDR.

Types of Troubled Debt Restructuring

The TDR sample contains 60 firms. Of these, three indicated intentions of debt restructuring in 1982 but had not yet entered into a TDR. Thirty-one (54.39 percent) of the remaining 57 TDR firms restructured their debt with a single type of restructuring or modification, while the remaining 26 firms (45.61 percent) used various combinations of terms. Six firms in this latter category did not specify their terms of restructuring. Therefore, 51 firms will be reviewed to determine the specific terms of the debt restructuring they underwent.

There were six basic types of TDR encountered in the sample: a reduction in principal, issuance of common stock for debt, issuance of preferred stock for debt, extension of maturity date, reduction in the interest rate, and reduction in accrued interest. See appendix C for a breakdown of the types of restructuring each firm used.

Representatives of two banks were interviewed to determine what steps they took when implementing a TDR. Those at the first bank said in almost all cases they prefer to defer the interest. In this manner, they will still get the full amount of principal and interest. If this fails, they then consider more lenient terms. However, at that point, they analyze each debtor firm individually so there is no fixed step-by-step process.

Those interviewed at the second bank cited several factors which influence a TDR. The most important factor was that the bank must be reasonably certain that the firm can increase its cash flow or working capital as a result of the TDR. Given this, the type of TDR is dependent upon the size of the loan, the type of business involved, the debtor's honesty, and the debtor's past history with its creditors.

If the business has influence in the community, the bank is more flexible in granting a TDR. The bank would be more willing to grant a reduction in principal or accrued interest in this case. If the firm produces a product with no demand, the bank might allow the firm to extend its maturity date, which is a much stricter form of TDR.

Communication between the bank and its customer is also an important factor. Big city banks and smaller community banks tend to differ. According to one banker, as long as there is a good line of communication, the community bank tends to be more flexible than the big city bank in granting TDRs. A community bank tends to feel more responsible to the needs of local business.

Twenty-five of the 51 firms (49.02 percent) implemented a reduction in principal either solely or with some other modification. Twenty-four firms (47.06 percent) issued either common or preferred stock in settlement of debt. Seventeen firms (33.33 percent) extended their maturity date. Finally, only 5 firms (9.8 percent) lowered their interest rate and 6 firms (11.77 percent) had their accrued interest reduced.

At this point it is worth looking for any relationships between the TDR firms' type of restructuring and their working capital positions. Working capital is analyzed in a later section of this chapter, but for now, it is important to understand that working capital was found to be a critical factor distinguishing the TDR firms from the bankrupt and nonbankrupt samples.

Before TDR, 40 firms experienced decreasing working capital. Of these firms, 20 implemented a reduction in principal while 18 issued either common or preferred stock. Only 2 of the firms with decreasing working capital prior to TDR entered into another type of restructuring. This is an indication that the financially worse off firms with decreasing working capital had entered into the more lenient forms of TDR.

After TDR, 13 firms reported decreasing working capital. Of these firms, 6 had reduced their principal while 5 had issued either common or preferred stock. So, after TDR, most of the firms with decreasing working capital were the ones implementing the lenient TDRs.

Thirty firms had experienced negative working capital prior to TDR. Of these firms, 14 had reduced their principal while 13 had issued either common or preferred stock. Only 3 had implemented another type of TDR.

After TDR, there remained 13 firms with negative working capital. Of these firms 6 had reduced their principal and 3 had issued either common or preferred stock.

Therefore we see that most of the firms which had reduced their principal or issued stock had decreasing and/or negative working capital. These firms, in general, were financially worse off than the other TDR firms studied. After TDR, the majority of firms experiencing decreasing and/or negative working capital were still these financially weak firms, although fewer in number. Therefore, the firms with the worst fund flow problems entered into the more lenient TDRs.

In summary, the most common types of debt restructurings occurring were either reductions in principal or issuance of common or preferred stock. Some of the firms implemented a TDR consisting of more than one modification. For that reason, the total number of firms listed above exceeds 60. It is unclear whether the type of TDR is related to the firms' financial positions. This relationship is addressed in a later section of this chapter.

When a firm encounters financial difficulty, a reduction in principal may be advantageous for the debtor firm. In this manner, a substantial amount of debt can be forgiven, making funds available for other purposes. However, the creditor must first agree to excuse some of the principal owed. In situations where a reduction in principal was not part of the TDR, the creditors may not have allowed it. The creditor wants to maximize its cash inflows, so, if it believed that the principal could in fact be completely paid off, it would not agree to a reduction in principal.

Even though a reduction in principal may eliminate some of the firm's debt, the firm itself must become profitable if it intends to continue as a going concern.

In a poorly managed company, a reduction in principal may only serve to prolong failure. So the TDR itself is one step a troubled firm takes when trying to turn itself around.

The issuance of common and preferred stock is a common event among the sample firms. By issuing shares of stock to its creditors, the TDR firm can relinquish its debt. At the same time, the creditors may receive this stock in full value of the outstanding debt. However, the stock may or may not stay at this value. If the debtor firm is facing bankruptcy, the possibility is good that the stock's price may drop substantially. If the creditor agrees to this type of restructuring, he assumes the risk while holding the stock, but if the TDR firm turns around and the stock price remains the same or increases, the creditor ultimately will do well. The creditor can sell the stock at an amount equal to or greater than the amount of restructured debt.

An extension of the maturity date, a reduction in the interest rate, and a reduction in accrued interest are used to a much lesser extent by the sample firms. These types of restructuring probably do not have as much impact on a troubled firm's financial position as other types. In these cases, the dollar amounts involved will probably be relatively small. These terms can substantially reduce the firm's cash outflows and expenses; therefore, the firm may have a stronger cash flow and working capital as a result of TDR. Income would also increase since interest expense would be decreasing. Therefore, these types of TDR are probably implemented if the creditor will not agree to a reduction in principal or issuance of stock.

However, these modifications of terms may be what the debtor firm wants. For example, a firm may take out a long-term loan when the interest rate is 18 percent. Subsequently, if the interest rate falls to 8 percent and the firm becomes unable to make the loan payments, a reduction in the interest rate may help.

Why does a firm choose a particular type of modification of terms in a TDR? A number of factors could be involved. First, the TDR firm's management must decide upon which type of TDR it wishes to undertake, but since management may not agree, some negotiation may be involved within the firm. But second and more important, the creditor firm must agree to the specific terms of the TDR. This process will involve negotiation between the debtor and creditor firms. So the type of restructuring implemented is in fact the result of the bargaining involved.

A worthy task for future research would be to use this same sample of TDR firms and ask each one how the terms of the TDR came about. Creditors of the more troubled firms may have been more willing to give up some of the principal in an effort to avoid a total loss. A study could compare levels of financial distress of TDR firms with types of TDR.

Characteristics of TDR Firms

In this section, descriptive information about TDR firms is presented. More specifically, financial variables used are analyzed for the TDR firms in order to compare and contrast these firms with the bankrupt and nonbankrupt samples.

For years prior to TDR, three financial statement items will be analyzed. They are earnings before interest and taxes (EBIT), retained earnings (RE), and total capital (TC). These items were chosen because they tend to differ the most between bankrupt and nonbankrupt firms. Income is an important factor in the failure process. Also, looking at a firm's retained earnings and total capital balances can determine if it has been ailing over time. So, by studying these items, we can see whether the TDR firms resemble bankrupt or nonbankrupt firms.

Also analyzed here are four financial ratios. They are earnings before interest and taxes/interest expense (EBIT/INT), working capital/total assets (WC/TA), current portion of long-term debt/total assets (CLTD/TA), and long-term debt/total liabilities (LTD/TL). These ratios are associated with the general areas of predictive ability in bankruptcy studies. They deal with liquidity, profitability, coverage, and other earnings relative to leverage measures, capitalization, and earnings variability. Therefore these ratios may also be key factors in studying TDR firms.

It should be noted at this point that the Z scores computed for the TDR firms resulted in a bimodal distribution which will be addressed further in chapter 5. For now, it is necessary to say that roughly half of the TDR sample was classified as bankrupt prior to TDR. These firms had negative Z scores. The other half of the sample classified as nonbankrupt with positive Z scores. So, to examine financial statement items and ratios, the TDR sample was divided into two groups to determine if there were any differences between the two groups. If dichotomies existed between the two groups, it might have been useful to treat them as two distinct groups. However, as can be seen from the results presented, there appeared to be no differences between the two groups, so they were analyzed together.

The first item observed was EBIT. Intuitively we expect a healthy firm to earn income annually and a troubled firm to incur losses. Since the TDR firms are having problems paying their debt, it might be expected that some of these firms are incurring losses. The following table shows the results for the 60 TDR firms for one, two, and three years prior to TDR.

	Positive EBIT	Sporadic EBIT	Negative EBIT	Total
Classified as Nonbankrupt	4	9	13	26
Classified as Bankrupt	9	16	9	34
Total	13	25	22	60

One might expect positive EBIT to be associated with positive Z scores and negative EBIT to be associated with negative Z scores; however, this was not the case. Of the 13 firms having positive EBIT, 69.23 percent had negative Z scores. And of the 22 firms with negative EBIT, 59.09 percent had positive Z scores.

This result indicates several things. First, analysis of TDR firms in general becomes difficult, since even though these firms are considered troubled, several of them did not report a negative EBIT for three years prior to TDR. This could mean that some of them are profitable firms which may just be experiencing a cash flow problem at the TDR date.

Second, 47 out of the 60 TDR firms reported sporadic or negative EBIT for three years prior to TDR. This, then, is strong evidence that these firms are in financial trouble. However, only 33 firms had negative Z scores prior to TDR. Why did the model not classify at least 47 firms as bankrupt? Possibly some of these firms with sporadic EBIT were not really troubled firms. Or, perhaps the MDA model computed is not totally reliable or is sample specific. It is for this reason that emphasis should be placed on both the descriptive data from these firms and the statistical testing of Z scores.

Because of these differences, further analysis of both the descriptive data and the statistical testing is warranted. Perhaps more descriptive analysis or different statistical tests might explain the differences found. Another explanation could be that the MDA model produces more conservative results than what the raw data appear to say. It may be too early in the failure process for the model to detect the signs. (In fact, a comparison of the MDA results and the descriptive results, presented later, supports the general reliability of the MDA model.)

Finally, the failure process may include TDRs but all TDRs may not be part of the failure process. In other words, a firm which is in the failure process may implement a TDR, but any given firm which implements a TDR may not be part of the failure process.

Of the 26 firms with positive Z scores, 4 (15.39 percent) had positive EBIT prior to TDR. This fact in itself is an indication that these firms are not doing well, despite their respective Z scores. Thirteen (50 percent) incurred losses in each year for three years prior to TDR. Finally, 9 (35.61 percent) experienced losses in at least one year for three years prior to TDR.

Of the firms with negative Z scores, 9 (26.47 percent) had positive EBIT and 9 (26.47 percent) had negative EBIT for each of three years prior to TDR. Sixteen (47.06 percent) incurred losses in at least one of the three years prior to TDR. From these results, there does not appear to be any substantial difference between the firms with positive Z scores and those with negative Z scores.

In total, then, 47 (78.33 percent) of these firms incurred losses in at least one year. This is fairly strong evidence that they are troubled firms starting through the failure process. Only 13 (21.67 percent) reported positive EBIT. That fact alone, though, does not mean that these are healthy firms.

Since 13 firms reported positive EBIT for three years prior to TDR, further analysis was conducted to determine which types of TDRs were implemented. The results are interesting and are presented in the following table.

It is most important that the least common types of TDR were a reduction in principal and a reduction in principal plus accrued interest. But among the entire group of 60 firms (appendix C), reduction in principal was the most common type

Type of TDR	Number of Firms
Reduction in Principal	1
Reduction in Principal Interest	1
Extension of Maturity Date	3
Issuance of Preferred Stock	3
Issuance of Common Stock	5
Total	13

of TDR. It appears that the creditors considered that 11 of these 13 firms were capable of repaying their debt so they did not offer a reduction in principal. This was not true of the more troubled firms.

The other three types of TDRs implemented within this group of firms put the creditor at less risk. Unless the stock price drops rapidly, the creditors will assume the full value of the outstanding debt. The creditors must have believed that these firms would continue to operate.

There is an explanation here for why these firms needed a TDR. It appears that these firms were experiencing cash flow problems. Eight of them experienced negative working capital prior to TDR, which supports the idea of a funds flow problem. This could be company specific or common to their entire industry.

With respect to specific ratios for the bankrupt, nonbankrupt, and TDR samples, the assumption can be made that the nonbankrupt firms have the strongest ratios and the bankrupt firms have the weakest. The TDR firms' ratios might be assumed to be between the bankrupt and nonbankrupt firms. This was the case with all of the ratios analyzed except for that of working capital/total assets (WC/TA). This ratio was lowest for the TDR sample, and will be discussed in more detail later. In fact, WC/TA was negative for the TDR firms and was positive for both the bankrupt and nonbankrupt firms. This is also an indication that the TDR firms had a serious funds flow problem which resulted in their not being able to pay their debt. The bankrupt firms may have a higher WC/TA ratio since the bankruptcy court in many cases forgives large amounts of debt in order to help these firms.

The next item for analysis is retained earnings (RE). A firm which was once healthy and reports a deficit in retained earnings is likely to be experiencing losses over a period of years. However, a new firm reporting a deficit may have incurred a loss in only one year since it would not have had the opportunity to accumulate retained earnings over a period of years. Nevertheless, a deficit in retained earnings is a clear indication of a financially troubled firm. The following table shows the results of the TDR firms' retained earnings.

	Positive RE	Negative RE	Total
Classified as Nonbankrupt	6	20	26
Classified as Bankrupt	10	24	34
Total	16	44	60

Again, it should be noted that there does not appear to be any difference between the firms possessing positive Z scores and those possessing negative Z scores. Therefore, only the totals will be discussed.

Sixteen (26.67 percent) of the firms reported positive retained earnings prior to TDR; however, this does not mean that these firms were healthy. The only conclusion that can be drawn is that these firms have had sufficient income to offset any accumulated losses incurred and dividends paid over their lives. Forty-four (73.33 percent) reported deficits in retained earnings prior to TDR. A deficit in retained earnings means that over the life of the firm, the losses incurred have been greater than any income earned. This again is a clear indication that these are troubled firms. Some are experiencing losses year after year as they proceed through the failure process. It should be noted here that, for three years prior to TDR, some of these firms shifted from positive retained earnings to negative retained earnings, but no firm shifted in the opposite direction. After TDR, three firms did shift from negative to positive retained earnings, indicating the firms had become profitable again. Since there were just a few firms involved, no conclusions can be drawn.

Next, total capital (TC) will be analyzed in the same manner as RE. When TC becomes negative, the firm is definitely in trouble, since its liabilities exceed its assets. The following table shows the results of the TDR firms' total capital.

	Positive TC	Negative TC	Total
Classified as Nonbankrupt	20	6	26
Classified as Bankrupt	18	16	34
Total	38	22	60

In this case, there is a difference between the positive and negative Z scores so they will be analyzed separately. Among the firms with positive Z scores, 20 (76.92 percent) reported positive TC while 6 (23.08 percent) reported negative TC. So most of these firms, even though they might be in financial distress, still have more assets than liabilities. Among the firms with negative Z scores, 18 (52.94 percent) reported positive TC while 16 (47.06 percent) reported negative TC. It is evident that, in general, the firms with positive Z scores are somewhat healthier than the firms with negative Z scores. So even though many of the firms with positive Z scores appear to be in financial trouble, the MDA model did not pick them up. This is a weakness in the bankruptcy prediction model which will be discussed in chapter 5.

Next, four financial ratios were analyzed for the TDR, bankrupt, and non-bankrupt samples in order to determine if any similarities or dissimilarities existed. Since most firms in the TDR sample were experiencing financial difficulties prior to TDR (as evidenced above), the TDR sample was not split in two for analysis. These four ratios were chosen because of their predictive power. They are earnings before interest and taxes/interest expense (EBIT/INT), working capital/total assets (WC/TA), current portion of long-term debt/total assets (CLTD/TA), and long-term debt/total liabilities (LTD/TL). Earnings, debt, and working capital can be factors which distinguish between healthy and troubled firms.

The failure process begins with operating results below expectations. As the failure process continues, the firm experiences deteriorating operating results year after year. Therefore an important variable to be analyzed here is earnings. Also appearing in the beginning of the failure process are nonpayment of dividends, net loss and negative cash flow trends. Again, there is support for an earnings variable to be analyzed. Analysis of a funds flow variable is also warranted. In this study working capital was selected as a funds flow variable. Altman (1977) found working capital to be a better predictor than cash. Later in the failure process come lowered bond ratings, debt accommodation, and loan default. These events support the analysis of both current and long-term debt, which are analyzed separately since they may produce different results.

These ratios were chosen for analysis because of the various financial data composing them. In the first ratio, income and interest expense are compared. Typically, a troubled firm would be earning lower profits, and thus have a lower net income. This could also cause a cash flow problem. Interest expense might also be higher for those firms in default, making EBIT/INT smaller.

The second ratio analyzes working capital. Since working capital represents funds in a business, this ratio might be expected to get smaller as a firm's financial position worsens. The third ratio is a measure of the firm's current portion of long-term debt to total assets. This ratio is important, since the current portion of long-term debt could change significantly as the result of a TDR. For example, if the TDR results in the long-term debt becoming currently due, this ratio will increase sharply. This occurred in a few cases in this study. The last ratio is a measure of the firm's long-term debt to total liabilities. This ratio may also be significant in distinguishing between samples, since long-term debt can be substantially reduced as the result of a TDR. The last two ratios are important here because the purpose of a TDR is to modify the long-term debt in some way.

The following table shows the means of each of these ratios for each of the three samples studied. The period of analysis was one year prior to TDR for the TDR firms and one year prior to bankruptcy for the bankrupt and matched non-bankrupt firms.

The results of the first ratio, EBIT/INT, are what might be expected. The TDR sample fell between the bankrupt and nonbankrupt samples, coming out higher

Ratio	Bankrupt Sample	TDR Sample	Nonbankrupt Sample
EBIT/INT	-.7673	.7478	7.5927
WC/TA	.2377	-.3061	.3531
CLTD/TA	.1775	.1299	.0627
LTD/TL	.5006	.4369	.6216

than the bankrupt firms and lower than the nonbankrupt firms. It should be noted here, though, that the TDR firms' EBIT/INT was much closer to the bankrupt firms' ratio.

Since EBIT has previously been analyzed, special attention should be focused on interest expense at this point. It might be expected that a firm entering into a TDR would have a considerably higher interest expense than an otherwise healthy firm; when a firm goes into default, interest still accrues on the debt. So, average interest expense/total debt was computed for the bankrupt-nonbankrupt, non-bankrupt, and TDR samples. The following results were obtained:

Sample	Average Interest Expense/Total Debt
Nonbankrupt	.0555
TDR	.1527
Bankrupt	.1824

This ratio was computed for one year prior to bankruptcy for the bankrupt and for the TDR sample. The results are interesting. The TDR sample had an average interest expense/total debt ratio higher than that of the nonbankrupt sample. But the TDR firms' ratio was lower than that of the bankrupt sample. The ratio for the TDR sample was in fact very close to that of the bankrupt sample. This is a clear indication that the TDR firms were experiencing an interest expense problem prior to TDR. Since these firms were experiencing both deteriorating results and this interest expense problem prior to TDR, the evidence suggests that these firms had entered the failure state.

The next ratio, WC/TA, did not have the results expected. The nonbankrupt sample had a higher WC/TA than the other samples. The bankrupt firms had the second highest WC/TA ratio, while the TDR firms had the lowest WC/TA and on average had negative working capital. As was mentioned previously, since the TDR firms could not pay their debt, it is obvious that they should be experiencing a severe funds flow problem. But the bankrupt firms may have previously entered into TDRs, thus obtaining temporary funds flow relief. Also the bankruptcy court in many cases releases the bankrupt firms from their obligation to repay their debt. In this manner the bankrupt firms are able to start over and try to become going concerns again.

In order to analyze working capital further, two approaches were taken. First, working capital before and after TDR was examined to determine whether it was increasing or decreasing during these periods. The firms with positive Z scores were segregated from those with negative Z scores to determine if any differences existed between the two groups. The results are shown in the following table.

		WC Before TDR		WC After TDR		Total	
Decreasing	Z-	21		9		30	
WC	Z+	19		4		23	
Subtotal			40		13		53
Increasing	Z-	11		12		23	
WC	Z+	7		12		19	
Subtotal			18		24		42
No Data Available			2		23		25
Total			60		60		120

As might be expected, most firms (68.97 percent) had decreasing WC before TDR, which provides evidence of a cash flow or funds problem. There appears to be no difference between the firms with positive Z scores and those with negative Z scores. After TDR, 64.86 percent of the firms available for analysis experienced an increase in working capital. Although many firms were lost after TDR because of lack of data, there is a definite change in the working capital trend after TDR. It appears that working capital may be a key factor in the development of TDR research.

Since the WC/TA ratio was negative on the average, the second approach determines the number of firms with positive and with negative working capital before and after TDR. Again, the firms with positive Z scores are reported separately from those with negative Z scores to determine if any differences exist. The following table shows the results.

These results again prove interesting. First, prior to TDR, 51.72 percent of the TDR sample had negative WC. After TDR, 35.14 percent of the firms analyzed had negative WC. Although no definitive conclusions can be drawn because of the loss of firms, this appears to be a drastic reduction. This could mean that the TDRs did help these firms. Again, there does not appear to be any substantial difference between the firms with positive Z scores and the firms with negative Z scores. For the rest, 48.28 percent of the firms had positive WC before TDR while 64.86 percent had positive WC after TDR, so there is an increase in positive WC here also.

		WC Before TDR		WC After TDR		Total	
Negative	Z-	12		8		20	
WC	Z+	18		5		23	
Subtotal			30		13		43
Positive	Z-	20		13		33	
WC	Z+	8		11		19	
Subtotal			28		24		52
No Data Available			2		23		25
Total			60		60		120

One other item is worth noting. For firms with positive Z scores, 8 had positive WC before TDR and 11 had positive WC after TDR. Since 21 firms were lost after TDR, the increase in the number of firms having positive WC is 17 percent higher. One explanation could be that these firms were initially healthy so that there was a higher probability that these firms would achieve positive WC faster than other firms. These firms had positive Z scores as computed by the MDA model. The model classified them as nonbankrupt. Since they appear to be, in fact, healthy, the MDA model is somewhat supported.

The third ratio, CLTD/TA, measures the proportion of long-term debt currently due. As might be expected again, the bankrupt firms had the highest CLTD/TA, followed by the TDR firms, and the nonbankrupt firms had the lowest. This can be explained by the fact that as a firm becomes troubled and cannot pay off its debt, the portion currently due becomes larger over time.

Finally, the last ratio, LTD/TL, is a measure of the portion of a firm's total debt that is long-term. It is not surprising that the nonbankrupt firms had the highest value here since their creditors are not as concerned with their ability to settle this debt. When a firm gets into financial difficulty, fewer creditors will be willing to lend to it on a long-term basis. This may be due to the banks' own financial analysis or lowered bond ratings. However, it is uncertain why the TDR firms had a smaller value than the bankrupt firms.

An explanation for this result could be that, as a TDR firm goes into default, more and more of its long-term debt becomes currently due, which would significantly reduce the LTD/TL ratio. This occurred with several of the firms in the TDR sample. The bankrupt firms' ratio may be higher because when the bankruptcy court eliminates the firm's long-term debt, total debt also decreases, which may not change the LTD/TL ratio significantly. Again, as mentioned earlier, this effect would tend to increase funds flow. Finally, the nonbankrupt firms are likely to have higher credit ratings which would enable them to use much more leverage.

Comparison of Two TDR Firms

The two firms' 10-K reports are used to examine key financial statement items indicating financial strengths or weaknesses. The notes to the financial statements are perused to get an overall view of the company. The two firms are the John F. Lawhon Furniture Company and the Lexicon Corporation. The first company entered into a TDR in 1981 and subsequently filed for Chapter XI bankruptcy later that year. The second company entered into its TDR in 1979, but still continues to operate as a going concern.

These two firms are part of the 60 firms comprising the TDR sample, which was obtained from DISCLOSURE, Inc. and includes all publicly traded firms disclosing a TDR. Unfortunately, the reliability of the sample is not without question, since it requires human manpower to scan the financial statements of every publicly traded company to segregate each disclosure. As was mentioned in chapter 1, a few firms initially appeared in the sample which had never entered into or disclosed a TDR. Likewise, it is probable that several TDR firms did not appear in the sample, especially since disclosure of a TDR may appear in various places in a firm's financial statements.

The two firms which were chosen for further analysis are representative of the TDR sample in different ways. For example, one firm later filed for bankruptcy as several other firms in the sample did, while the other did not. The firms entered into different forms of TDR, but each of the TDR terms was common to several of the firms in the sample. One firm is an established firm, while the other one was a young, unestablished firm. The TDR sample contained several young, unestablished companies as well as some established ones. The John F. Lawhon Furniture Company experienced negative Z scores right up to bankruptcy while the Lexicon Corporation experienced declining positive Z scores prior to TDR. Since the distribution of firms was bimodal, the two firms fell into different groups; therefore, each is representative of several of the firms in its respective group.

John F. Lawhon Furniture Company

The John F. Lawhon Furniture Company (JFLF) is a retail furniture and bedding outlet. The company sells nationally advertised brands of furniture at discount prices. Composed of ten facilities within seven states, the company caters to customers in the low and middle income brackets.

Since merchandise is sold at discount prices, the customers either assume the responsibility of picking up the furniture themselves or pay additional delivery charge fees. This delivery revenue is insignificant for the company. Another source of insignificant revenue is the company's subsidiary, which sells damaged and repossessed inventory. Therefore, the major revenues of the JFLF Company come from new furniture sales.

In order to offer discount prices, the company purchases inventory in large quantities, usually in railroad or truckload lots. Because of this purchase strategy, customers are able to receive about 90 percent of their purchased merchandise immediately. However, the company must maintain high levels of merchandise inventory, which ties up cash normally available for other purposes.

The retail furniture industry is highly competitive. Competitors include other retail furniture outlets along with department and discount stores. The JFLF Company recognized that some of its competitors had greater resources, either financial or other, which put the JFLF Company at a disadvantage. Other factors affecting operations are high interest rates, credit restrictions, inflation, and a decline in economic conditions.

In 1976, the company suffered a net loss but had sales of over 20 million dollars. In 1977, revenues rose by 6 million dollars and the company earned a profit. The increase in profits continued into 1978, where net income almost doubled from 1977. In these three years, the cost of goods sold and selling and administrative expenses increased with revenues. However, interest expense declined 4 percent in 1977 and 2 percent in 1978.

In 1979, revenues increased by 56 percent. This substantial increase was due to several new store openings. Cost of goods sold, which remained around 60 percent of sales for 1976, 1977, and 1978, was reduced only slightly in 1979 to 59 percent. Selling expenses as a percentage of sales increased by 3 percent in 1979 to 38 percent. Again, the new store openings were primarily responsible for this increase.

Interestingly, the company's interest expense, which was on a downward trend, jumped by 30 percent in 1979. This substantial increase was caused both by an increase in interest rates and an increase in outstanding debt. As a result of these factors, the company reported a net loss in 1979. The costs of new store openings in that year had a major impact on these results.

In 1980, there were no new store openings. Revenues increased only slightly, while at the same time, the nation experienced a decline in the general economy. Cost of goods sold as a percentage of sales dropped by 2 percent, but selling and administrative costs as a percentage of sales increased by 1 percent. Again in 1980, interest expense increased by 82 percent from 1979. This severe increase was again due to an increase in interest rates and an increase in outstanding debt. Despite this unfavorable increase, the company reported positive net income in 1980.

As the TDR date approaches, a few things are noteworthy. First, revenues, cost of goods sold, and selling and administrative expenses tend to be changing only slightly. As revenues increase, so do the expenses, but they remain fairly constant as a percentage of those revenues. This is similar to the figures in a healthy firm. Second, interest expense in the previous two years has increased dramatically, more than doubling each year. This may indicate a debt problem for the company. Finally, net income and loss reported each year seem to sway back and forth with no trend. Although there is no downward trend here, it certainly is not the sign of a healthy company.

Early in fiscal 1981, the company was suffering from the same problem it had before the economy declined and interest rates reached a record high. A serious cash flow problem caused action to be taken—the TDR. The company also began to close some of its unprofitable stores in that year.

At the end of fiscal 1981 the company entered into a TDR where it extended the 1981 maturities of its long-term debt over the next five-year period. No mention was made about how this TDR was negotiated with the creditors, so it is impossible to determine how long the TDR negotiation took and how different the TDR terms were from what the company had initially wanted.

The company reported its highest net loss ever in fiscal 1981, over six million dollars. Revenues and costs decreased as a result of the store closings, but interest expense remained constant.

In the beginning of fiscal 1982, the JFLF Company filed for bankruptcy under Chapter XI of the National Bankruptcy Act. At this point the firm went under reorganization and the TDR became irrelevant. During fiscal 1982, the company continued closing unprofitable stores. As a result, revenues decreased in 1982, as did expenses. Interest expense dropped by 60 percent as a result of the reorganization. Finally, the firm reported income before extraordinary items and an extraordinary gain from debt restructuring under bankruptcy reorganization. It appears at this point that the company may again become a going concern and avoid liquidation.

A few other items should be examined for this company during this period. From 1979 to 1982, total assets decreased as a result of poor operations and store closings. Current liabilities remained fairly constant until 1982, when they were substantially reduced. Long-term debt was reduced again. The retained earnings deficit was substantially reduced as a result of the bankruptcy proceedings. Finally, in each year prior to 1982, the company showed a decrease in working capital, but as a result of the reorganization, it experienced an increase in working capital for fiscal 1982 of almost six million dollars.

At this point, a natural question arises: Why was the TDR not effective for the JFLF Company? There may be many factors contributing to the answer, a few of which seem readily apparent.

The period of time between the TDR and bankruptcy was less than one year, so it may have been too late for the company to restructure its debt at that point. If the company had undertaken a TDR when it first experienced a loss in 1976, it might have been successful. Why did it not do this? Perhaps management did not feel it was necessary. Perhaps the creditors would not agree. It seems likely, though, that the need for a TDR should have been evident earlier, and perhaps earlier implementation could have avoided bankruptcy.

Another question arises: Could implementation of a more lenient TDR have enabled JFLF to avoid bankruptcy? Although it is impossible to answer that question at this point, the company appears to be turning into a profitable concern again after bankruptcy. Could a different TDR have accomplished the same result? The JFLF Company's TDR was for an extension of its maturity date only. Suppose, for example, that the TDR had called for a substantial reduction in principal; it appears that this type of TDR might have been more helpful than an extension of maturity date. Why, then, did the company not implement a reduction in principal? The answer again is unknown. Perhaps management tried for a reduction in principal but the creditors would not allow it, or management did not feel the company was in as bad a position as it actually was. These unanswered but interesting questions may be addressed by future research studies.

In conclusion, the lack of success of the TDR implemented by the JFLF Company might have been avoided by better timing or by implementing a different type of TDR. It is also possible that the failure of the TDR was inevitable.

The Lexicon Corporation

The Lexicon Corporation is a manufacturer of an electronic hand-held language translator. The company was incorporated in 1976 and remained in the development stages until November 1978. At that time, the company began sales of its product. In October 1979, the company entered into a TDR which essentially was a reduction in principal.

In August 1979, the company contracted with a private manufacturer and granted the manufacturer the exclusive worldwide license to manufacture, assemble, and market the company's products. The manufacturer agreed to attempt to sell all of the company's inventories.

In 1981, the company again entered into a TDR. This TDR also called for a reduction in principal. It should be noted that the company still had not achieved profitability as of December 1981.

In 1982, the company was producing two major products—the LEX-21 computer terminal and the LEX-31 personal communications computer. During the first six months of 1982, sales of these products increased significantly. Also in 1982, Bytec Management Corporation purchased a large portion of Lexicon's stock, making more capital available. The company planned to finance any additional expenditures through the issuance of equity securities.

It is interesting to note that, until 1982, a significant portion of the company's financing was accomplished through the use of long-term debt. It was not until 1982 that the undercapitalized firm began to issue additional stock to obtain needed capital. Lexicon may have been restricted by its outstanding creditors.

For the first six months of fiscal 1982, product sales of Lexicon increased 53 percent over the first six months of fiscal 1981. Although the company was still having financial problems, its substantial increase in revenues indicates that it had good growth potential. This factor surely must have been recognized by the firm's creditors when granting the TDRs.

From the start of operations in 1976, total assets of the company increased in each year except 1980. However, in 1981, total assets reached a new peak. They were 327 percent over 1980 and 73 percent over 1979. For the first time in the history of its operations, the retained earnings deficit did not increase significantly. This was due to the $7,000 net loss reported in 1981, the lowest loss in its history. Long-term debt reached its highest point in 1979 and began to decrease substantially thereafter. Interest expense followed the same pattern. In fact, long-term debt decreased by 54 percent in 1981 and interest expense by 83 percent.

Selling expenses increased significantly in 1982 due to advertising costs for the LEX-21 and LEX-31. Also, the marketing group increased its staff. These costs aimed at increasing sales for 1982 and future years. General and administrative expenses increased by 35 percent in 1982. This increase was due to settlement of a lawsuit, higher costs of stock tradings, higher allowance for uncollectible accounts, and increases in professional fees.

Overall, Lexicon Corporation was making progress through its increased sales. The expenses related to these sales had also increased, but the company had specifically traced and indicated the reasons for the increased expenses, which seem to be reasonable. It appeared that the company was keeping a very close watch over its operations. Creditors would find this to be a positive factor when considering whether or not to grant a TDR.

Finally, the company predicted a promising year in fiscal 1983. It forecast increased sales of the LEX-21 and LEX-31. There may also be an opportunity for the company to become involved with government research and development which would lead to a significant increase from government sales.

The Lexicon Corporation is a fairly new company and not without the financial problems encountered by almost all new companies. In 1979, its creditors granted it a reduction in principal. The question arises: Did the TDR help the firm? To answer this question, earnings before interest and taxes (EBIT) need to be examined. The EBIT for 1977 was −$108,000 and in 1978 was −$286,000. By 1979, the company reached its highest net loss ever, which amounted to −$2,014,000. After the TDR in 1979, the EBIT went to −$265,000 in 1980, much better than in 1979, but the firm was still operating at a loss. So the TDR in 1979 may have helped the company to turn in the right direction by reducing its annual losses. Of course, other factors may have contributed to this reversal. At that point, sales increased, which would contribute to the reduction in losses. This is not unusual for a new company.

Evidently, though, the 1979 TDR was not sufficient, since the company again entered into a TDR in 1981, when the creditors granted the company another reduction in principal. Did this TDR help the Lexicon Corporation? By 1981, Lexicon was marketing the LEX-21 and began to increase its sales significantly. The EBIT for 1981 was only −$7,000, a substantial decrease from prior years. Fiscal 1982 operations were promising, although a loss was still reported in the quarterly statements. There are so many unknown factors here that it is impossible to answer the questions, but the fact that the company has remained in operation is an indication that the TDR helped. By reducing the principal of its long-term debt, the company was able to meet the obligations of its creditors. If there were no TDR, there would have been a great probability of the Lexicon Corporation's going into default and Chapter XI bankruptcy.

Why did the creditors agree to a second TDR when the first one apparently was not successful? They must have believed that the company had good potential for becoming successful and were willing to bend more than with a firm they believed could not become profitable. Why did the creditors allow a reduction in principal both times? If they were confident of the company's future success, certainly an extension of maturity date would have been more beneficial to them. Once again, this question cannot be answered with certainty. However, they must have felt that the principal was too much of a financial burden for the company.

Future research can try to find the answers to these questions. A questionnaire-type study could ask each of the TDR firms these unanswered questions.

Comparison

The two firms analyzed in this chapter, the John F. Lawhon Furniture Company and the Lexicon Corporation, are quite different, but they have one thing in common—they have both restructured their debt. The JFLF Company was a profitable operation at one time which later entered into Chapter XI bankruptcy. The Lexicon Corporation was a new company still trying to get off the ground. The firms used different types of TDR. One used an extension of maturity date while the other used a reduction in principal. Finally, the TDR was unsuccessful for the JFLF Company while Lexicon's might prove to be successful.

The explanations for the success and failure of these TDRs are so numerous that it is impossible to pinpoint them exactly. The firms themselves are very different, their creditors are different, and the type of TDRs they used are different. Future research can address itself to these problems.

Summary

In this chapter several aspects of TDR firms have been analyzed. Thirty-one out of 60 TDR firms used only one type of restructuring while the others used more than one type. Twenty-five firms entered into a reduction of principal, 24 issued either common or preferred stock, 17 extended their maturity date, 5 lowered their interest rate, and 6 reduced their accrued interest. The financially worse off firms (with decreasing and negative working capital) tended to use the more lenient forms of TDRs such as a reduction in principal or issuance of stock. There were 13 firms which appeared to be healthy. These tended to use the stricter forms of TDR such as extension of maturity date.

EBIT, RE, and TC were analyzed before TDR. It was found that most firms were experiencing losses in at least one year prior to TDR. This result supports the theory that TDR is part of the failure process. Also, several firms had negative

RE and TC, which indicates recurring losses from year to year. Again, this gives further support for including TDR as part of the failure process.

Four financial ratios were analyzed. As might be expected, the nonbankrupt firms had the strongest ratios while the bankrupt firms had the weakest. The one exception was WC/TA, where the TDR sample had the lowest. This result indicates a serious funds flow problem for the TDR firms. The bankrupt firms had a higher WC/TA, probably either from previous TDRs or bankruptcy reorganization.

There was a trend for TDR firms with decreasing working capital prior to TDR to shift toward increasing working capital after TDR. There was also a trend for these firms to shift from negative working capital prior to TDR to positive working capital after TDR.

Finally, two TDR firms were analyzed in more detail. The JFLF Company extended its maturity date and later filed for bankruptcy. The Lexicon Corporation reduced its principal and still continues to operate as a going concern.

5

Empirical Results of the Model

Sample Selection

The sample of bankrupt firms consists of 35 firms which filed for Chapter X or XI under the National Bankruptcy Act between 1972 and 1981. In addition to this characteristic, the firms were listed on the COMPUSTAT Industrial Research File, which facilitated the data-gathering process. Selected data were extracted for one, two, and three years prior to bankruptcy in order to develop the discriminant bankruptcy model. Data for three years prior to bankruptcy were available for all 35 firms, but data were only available for 32 and 27 firms for two years and one year prior to bankruptcy, respectively. The missing data illustrate a major weakness of the COMPUSTAT tapes.

The firms comprising the nonbankrupt sample were matched by industry and size of total assets and revenues to their bankrupt counterparts. In this manner, each matched pair was as similar as possible, with the exception of their bankruptcy status. Each firm in the nonbankrupt sample was also listed on the COMPUSTAT Industrial File. Selected data were extracted for each of these 35 firms in order to develop the discriminant bankruptcy model.

The debt-restructured sample consisted of 60 firms which disclosed some form of TDR in their 1981 financial statements. Variables were computed for each of these firms in order to evaluate them with the discriminant model. The twelve discriminating variables derived from the MDA bankruptcy model which will be discussed later in this chapter were selected for analysis. The variables were computed for one, two, and three years prior to restructuring. In addition, ratios were computed for the year of restructuring and for each year after restructuring.

Variable Selection

Selected financial ratios were chosen for discriminating variables. Using financial statement items considered to be significant by the Altman Zeta model (1977), 25 financial ratios were derived (see appendix B). These ratios were computed for each firm in the bankrupt and nonbankrupt samples for one, two, and three years prior to bankruptcy. The ratios were then analyzed by the multiple discriminant analysis package MULDIS to determine those ratios which had the most predictive power.

Multiple Discriminant Analysis

A bankruptcy prediction model was developed using MDA. The two qualitative discrete groups were the sample of bankrupt and the sample of nonbankrupt firms. The characteristics or variables were the 25 financial ratios selected for analysis.

It is not clear that the variables selected for the MDA model do not arise from multivariate normal populations and, accordingly, this factor was cited in the limitations section in chapter 1. However, MDA has been found to be a robust test, even when the normality requirement is violated (Eisenbeis and Avery, 1972). From the discriminant function computed, it was found that the variance-covariance matrices were not equal and that variables did not have a normal distribution. Linear MDA was found to classify with the best accuracy and so was used for this study. Linear MDA has been found to have very good classification accuracy in similar studies (Altman, 1977; Rose and Giroux, 1980).

MDA selects the most significant financial ratios of the matched firms which best classify the firms in their respective groups. In this study, MULDIS selected the ratios which best classified the bankrupt and nonbankrupt firms into their bankrupt and nonbankrupt categories. Of the 25 variables used for selection, MULDIS selected the 12 which best classified the two groups. Appendix B lists all 25 variables used and the 12 selected for the discriminant model. The F-statistics and percent of discriminating power of the 12 variables are also shown in appendix B.

MULDIS selects the best set of discriminating variables where Wilks' lambda is minimized. Wilks' lambda was at a minimum in the best 12 variable set, equal to .1891203. Of the variables selected, 6 deal with liquidity and income items. The remaining 6 deal with either current or long-term debt. This result makes intuitive sense, since bankrupt firms are generally distinguished by net losses and liquidity problems.

For variable selection, MULDIS has several options available. They include complete, forward, and backward stepwise selection procedures. All three options were tested for completeness. Using each of the three options available, the same 12 variables were selected. However, slightly different coefficients and percent of discriminating power were computed for each variable. But the equation developed under each option classified the same number of firms correctly, implying that there are no significant differences among the three options using this data.

Multiple Discriminant Analysis Results

Four different MDA functions were computed. One function was computed for the samples one year prior to bankruptcy, another was computed for two years prior to bankruptcy, and a third was computed for three years prior to bankruptcy. Finally, an MDA function was computed for all three years prior to bankruptcy combined together.

The best classification results were obtained for one year prior to bankruptcy. This result makes intuitive sense, since the closer to bankruptcy a firm comes, the more discriminating its predictor variables should be, because its financial position is worsening. This result is consistent with previous studies (Altman, 1977; Rose and Giroux, 1980). Therefore, the MDA function computed for one year prior to bankruptcy is used to evaluate the TDR firms.

The ratios selected for the MDA model and their discriminating power are listed in table 4. The first ratio, as mentioned earlier, is a measure of working capital or funds, which should be an important ratio for a TDR firm, since the TDR firms are lacking funds to settle their debt.

Table 4

Ratios Selected for the Discriminant Function

Ratio		Percent of Discriminating Power
1.	Working Capital/Total Assets	10.073 43%
2.	Income Before Extraordinary Items/Total Assets	3.322073%
3.	Earnings Before Interest and Taxes/Total Assets	.3233316%
4.	Earnings Before Interest and Taxes/Interest Expense	4.523617%
5.	Current Assets/Total Assets	7.076948%
6.	Current Liabilities/Total Assets	.2482795%
7.	Earnings Before Taxes/Total Assets	1.964262%
8.	Current Long-term Debt/Total Assets	5.217768%
9.	Current Long-term Debt/Current Assets	6.265601%
10.	Long-term Debt/Total Capital	16.36950%
11.	Long-term Debt/Common Equity	27.07425%
12.	Long-term Debt/Total Liabilities	17.54093%
	Total	99.99999%

Ratios 2-4 and 7 are measures of income. Income before extraordinary items includes interest expense and income taxes expense. However, earnings before interest and taxes (EBIT) does not take these expenses into account. One of these ratios measures EBIT as a percent of interest expense. Interest expense is also an important item, since a TDR deals directly with debt and interest.

The fifth and sixth ratios selected analyze the firms' current assets and current liabilities, respectively. These ratios, as a percent of total assets, measure the proportion of the firms' balance sheet that is current. Although similar to working capital, these ratios analyze current assets and current liabilities individually.

The eighth and ninth ratios are measures of the firms' current portion of long-term debt, while the last three ratios measure the firms' long-term debt. As we mentioned previously, long-term debt is very significant as it relates to TDRs. This can be seen directly, as the discriminating power of these last three ratios is 60.98 percent. The current portion of long-term debt is also important, since this is the portion of the firms' debt that they cannot pay. The discriminating power of these two ratios is 11.49 percent.

The results of this discriminant function can be condensed as shown in table 2 (p. 34). This table indicates the correctly and incorrectly classified firms. A bankrupt firm which classified as nonbankrupt is called a Type I error while a nonbankrupt firm which classified as bankrupt is called a Type II error. Table 5 shows the results of the discriminant function by number of firms and percent of total.

The linear function classified 92.593 percent of the bankrupt firms correctly and 96.296 percent of the nonbankrupt firms correctly. The quadratic function classified 96.296 percent of the bankrupt firms correctly but only 85.185 percent of the nonbankrupt firms correctly. Other studies have also shown that linear MDA performs better than quadratic MDA in bankruptcy studies (Rose and Giroux, 1980; Altman et al., 1977).

Table 5 shows the results of both functions one year prior to bankruptcy. Table 6 shows the results of the other three functions computed but not used here. In these years, the percent of classification accuracy varied from a high of 81.25 percent to a low of 45.714 percent. While 81.25 percent is much better than chance, 45.714 percent is a very poor classification accuracy.

The percent of correctly classified firms drops significantly for two years and three years prior to bankruptcy. Due to this fact, these functions were not used here. It might be argued that since a TDR occurs prior to bankruptcy, these models might be more reliable for analyzing the TDR firms. However, since this study investigates the relationship between TDR firms and bankrupt firms, the model just prior to bankruptcy is used, since it best characterizes the bankrupt firms.

The linear function better classified both groups, so it is used to evaluate the TDR firms. The MDA function computes a Z score for each observation. This score is the result of multiplying the given observation ratios by the MDA function coefficients and then summing. A critical Z score (Zc) is determined, where Z scores falling above Zc are classified as nonbankrupt and scores falling below are classified as bankrupt. The Zc score used in the MULDIS package is zero. Table 7 shows how each of the TDR firms was classified before and after TDR based upon its Z scores in those years.

Table 5

MDA Results—One Year Prior to Bankruptcy

Linear Classification

(Lachenbruch Holdout Method)

Predicted

Actual	Bankrupt	Nonbankrupt	Total
Bankrupt	25	2	27
Nonbankrupt	1	26	27
Column Total	26	28	54

Percent Table of Linear Classification

Predicted

Actual	Bankrupt	Nonbankrupt	Total
Bankrupt	92.593%	7.407%	100%
Nonbankrupt	3.704%	96.296%	100%
Column Average	48.148%	51.852%	100%

Quadratic Classification -One Year Prior to Bankruptcy

Predicted

Actual	Bankrupt	Nonbankrupt	Total
Bankrupt	26	1	27
Nonbankrupt	4	23	27
Column Total	30	24	54

Percent Table of Quadratic Classification

Predicted

Actual	Bankrupt	Nonbankrupt	Total
Bankrupt	96.296%	3.704%	100%
Nonbankrupt	14.815%	85.185%	100%
Column Average	55.556%	44.444%	100%

Table 6
MDA Results—Several Years Prior to Bankruptcy

Three Years Prior to Bankruptcy
Linear Classification
(Lachenbruch Holdout Method)

Predicted

Actual	Bankrupt	Nonbankrupt	Total
Bankrupt	18	17	35
Nonbankrupt	11	24	35
Column Total	29	41	70

Percent Table of Linear Classification

Predicted

Actual	Bankrupt	Nonbankrupt	Total
Bankrupt	51.429%	48.571%	100%
Nonbankrupt	31.429%	68.571%	100%
Column Average	41.429%	58.571%	100%

Quadratic Classification

Predicted

Actual	Bankrupt	Nonbankrupt	Total
Bankrupt	27	8	35
Nonbankrupt	19	16	35
Column Total	46	24	70

Percent Table of Quadratic Classification

Predicted

Actual	Bankrupt	Nonbankrupt	Total
Bankrupt	77.143%	22.857%	100%
Nonbankrupt	54.286%	45.714%	100%
Column Average	65.714%	34.286%	100%

Table 6 (continued)

Two Years Prior to Bankruptcy
Linear Classification
(Lachenbruch Holdout Method)

Predicted

Actual	Bankrupt	Nonbankrupt	Total
Bankrupt	21	11	32
Nonbankrupt	8	24	32
Column Total	29	35	64

Percent Table of Linear Classification

Predicted

Actual	Bankrupt	Nonbankrupt	Total
Bankrupt	65.625%	34.375%	100%
Nonbankrupt	25 %	75 %	100%
Column Average	45.313%	54.688%	100%

Quadratic Classification

Predicted

Actual	Bankrupt	Nonbankrupt	Total
Bankrupt	26	6	32
Nonbankrupt	10	22	32
Column Total	36	28	64

Percent Table of Quadratic Classification

Predicted

Actual	Bankrupt	Nonbankrupt	Total
Bankrupt	81.25 %	18.75 %	100%
Nonbankrupt	31.25 %	68.75 %	100%
Column Average	56.25 %	43.75 %	100%

Table 6 (continued)

One, Two, and Three Years Prior to Bankruptcy Combined
Linear Classification
(Lachenbruch Holdout Method)

Predicted

Actual	Bankrupt	Nonbankrupt	Total
Bankrupt	67	20	87
Nonbankrupt	21	66	87
Column Total	88	86	174

Percent Table of Linear Classification

Predicted

Actual	Bankrupt	Nonbankrupt	Total
Bankrupt	77.011%	22.989%	100%
Nonbankrupt	24.138%	75.862%	100%
Column Average	50.575%	49.425%	100%

Quadratic Classification

Predicted

Actual	Bankrupt	Nonbankrupt	Total
Bankrupt	64	23	87
Nonbankrupt	18	69	87
Column Total	82	92	174

Percent Table of Quadratic Classification

Predicted

Actual	Bankrupt	Nonbankrupt	Total
Bankrupt	73.563%	26.437%	100%
Nonbankrupt	20.69 %	79.31 %	100%
Column Average	47.126%	52.874%	100%

Table 7
MDA Results of TDR Firms

Classification	Results of the TDR Firms					
	Bankrupt	%	Nonbankrupt	%	Total	%
Three years prior to TDR	29	55.77	23	44.23	52	100
Two years prior to TDR	23	40.35	34	59.65	57	100
One year prior to TDR	30	50.00	30	50.00	60	100
Year of TDR	33	56.90	25	43.10	58	100
One year after TDR	25	58.14	18	41.86	43	100
Two years after TDR	9	36.00	16	64.00	25	100
Three years after TDR	4	44.44	5	55.56	9	100

The TDR sample consists of large firms with total assets over one million dollars. All of the bankrupt and nonbankrupt firms also had total assets over one million dollars. The TDR firms are all industrial and retail firms which are similar in industry codes to the bankrupt and nonbankrupt samples. There are several different industries represented in each sample, so the model should not be industry specific. The firms in all three samples are scattered throughout the United States.

The centroid for the nonbankrupt group is very close to zero. This might be an indication either that the nonbankrupt sample does not contain healthy firms or that there are a few nonbankrupt firms which are not strong, causing the nonbankrupt centroid to be close to the bankrupt centroid. Nevertheless, the function classified significantly better than chance for one year prior to bankruptcy.

A major factor to be considered here is which MDA model is appropriate for evaluation of the TDR firms. It could be argued that since the TDR event occurs prior to the bankruptcy event, one of the discriminant functions prior to bankruptcy would be appropriate. In this particular study, the MDA model for one year prior to bankruptcy had good classification results, but those models beyond one year prior to bankruptcy had very poor results (see table 6 for a breakdown of results for each model). For example, for two years prior to bankruptcy, the linear function classified 65.625 percent of the bankrupt firms correctly and 75 percent of the nonbankrupt firms correctly. The quadratic function classified 81.25 percent and 68.75 percent of these firms correctly, respectively. The best classification result for three years prior to bankruptcy was in the quadratic function. This function classified 77.143 percent of the bankrupt firms correctly but only 45.714 percent of the nonbankrupt firms correctly. Using all three years prior to bankruptcy, correct classification results ranged from 73 percent to 79 percent.

In this study, then, the model for one year prior to bankruptcy is used to evaluate the TDR firms. This function also best discriminates between the bankrupt and nonbankrupt firms just before bankruptcy and, since part of the study compares the bankrupt and TDR firms, this model is the best for distinguishing between the two samples.

Z scores were computed for each of the TDR firms. Non-parametric statistical tests are performed from these Z scores in order to evaluate the TDR firms. This methodology has been used to measure the firms' systematic risk based on Z scores (Altman and Brenner, 1981). As a firm's Z score changes from nonbankrupt to bankrupt, the systematic risk in its stock price might be expected to rise.

Altman and Brenner studied the effect on stock prices of newly reported financial data. Previous studies in this area (which are referred to as efficient market hypothesis studies) have concluded that newly reported financial data are already incorporated into the stock price so that an investor cannot earn excessive profits from this new information.

Previous studies used the capital asset pricing model to measure a given stock's rate of return. In their study, Altman and Brenner incorporated the newly reported financial data into Altman's 1968 MDA bankruptcy prediction model to create new information. They computed Z scores for each firm and used firms which had shifted Z scores between the bankrupt and nonbankrupt categories. Finally, they computed the firms' systematic risk before and after the change in Z scores. The change in Z scores was used to determine if there were changes in the stock prices due to new information. They had some evidence to conclude that the change in Z scores did not affect the stock price. In other words, this new information (the change in Z scores) was already incorporated into the stock price. In the present study the Z scores of the TDR firms are also used for analysis of the firms' financial positions.

The results of the non-parametric statistical tests are presented later in this chapter. The variables used for evaluation were those which best discriminated between bankrupt and nonbankrupt firms one year prior to bankruptcy. Since TDR is assumed to be a pre-bankruptcy event as part of the failure process, these variables are appropriate for evaluation of the TDR firms.

The linear discriminant function had good classification accuracy for one year prior to bankruptcy (table 5). It classified 92.593 percent of the bankrupt firms correctly, resulting in a 7.407 percent Type I error. Nonbankrupt firms were classified with 96.296 percent accuracy, resulting in a 3.704 percent Type II error. Therefore, this linear equation is the one used to evaluate the TDR firms.

Analysis of TDR Firms

Using the linear discriminant function derived from MULDIS, Z scores were computed for each of the 60 TDR firms. Where data were available, a Z score was computed for each firm for three, two, and one year prior to TDR, the year of

TDR, and one, two, and three years after TDR. A Z score above zero places the firm into the nonbankrupt category while a Z score below zero places the firm into the bankrupt category. Table 7 shows the classification results of the TDR firms for each year.

For the firms classifying as nonbankrupt in each year, about two-thirds had Z scores greater than 10, which indicates that they were profitable or similar to the nonbankrupt firms. The highest Z scores are an indication of the healthiest firms. The Z score distribution is an ordinal ranking which merely classifies firms from lowest to highest Z scores. The lowest scores are the financially worst off firms while the highest scores are the healthiest firms. Firms with Z scores close to Zc are considered to be in an overlap area, not very healthy and not very unhealthy. Only five firms had Z scores between zero and four. These few firms, although classifying as nonbankrupt, were close to the cutoff point. Therefore, these firms might, in fact, be troubled.

Of the firms classified as bankrupt in each year, about half had Z scores less than −10, which is an indication that they were in financially vulnerable positions. Very low Z scores are an indication of very troubled firms. Only a few firms had Z scores between −4 and 0, which would fall into the overlap area. Most firms classified as bankrupt had Z scores between −4 and −10. These Z scores result in a bimodal distribution, since the majority of firms classified as nonbankrupt fall at one end of the continuum while the majority of firms classified as bankrupt lie at the opposite end.

Prior to TDR, about half of the firms were classified as bankrupt. This bimodal distribution indicates that all of the firms may not be following through the failure process, although those firms classifying as bankrupt appear to be doing so. Those firms classifying as nonbankrupt may not be in the failure process at all, or they may be deteriorating as part of the failure process but their financial positions may not be weak enough to classify them as bankrupt. After TDR, there is no shift of firms from the bankrupt to nonbankrupt category; however, a more detailed analysis of how each individual firm changes from year to year will indicate if the TDR has had any effect on the firm's financial position. Statistical testing of the Z score results can achieve this need. Even though half of these firms had positive Z scores, a significant decline in Z scores for each year prior to TDR may be an indication that they are in fact following the failure process.

Although only about half of the firms classified as bankrupt prior to TDR, 52 of them (86.67 percent) experienced net losses in one or more years prior to TDR. Twenty-two of the 60 TDR firms reported deficit balances for total equity prior to restructuring. Of these 22, 16 had negative Z scores, while 6 had positive Z scores. These results indicate that, in general, these firms were having financial difficulties prior to TDR.

It is also interesting to note that 44 firms in the TDR sample reported deficit balances in retained earnings prior to restructuring. These negative trends are an indication that their financial positions were deteriorating before the TDR date.

Most of them had deficits in retained earnings, while some reported deficits for total equity. Therefore, these firms in general seem to be following through the failure process. The fact that about half of these firms had positive Z scores for three years prior to TDR might indicate that the bankruptcy prediction model is not reliable for a distant time period before TDR in the failure process. From the detailed analysis of these firms (presented in chapter 4), there appears to be some support for the MDA model computed.

In chapter 4, it was found that funds flow was a critical factor distinguishing the TDR firms. The ratios selected in the MDA model which contain working capital items account for 28.88203 percent of its discriminating power. So in both cases, working capital was a significant distinguishing item.

Results of Statistical Testing

The results of Z scores of the TDR firms fell into a bimodal distribution. That distribution is shown in figure 2. Had the Z scores resulted in a normal distribution, parametric statistical tests would have been appropriate. A normal distribution would have looked like figure 3.

Figure 2

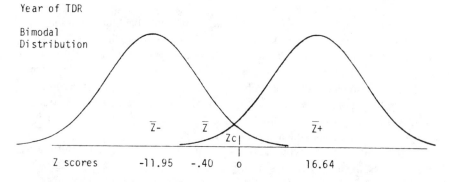

In figure 2, the overlap area in the center represents a range of Z scores where it is uncertain whether the firms should be classified as bankrupt or nonbankrupt. The Z score distribution is a continuum, with zero being an arbitrary cutoff point. Firms with Z scores very close to zero are difficult to classify; they are not healthy firms with a Z score over 10, nor are they very sick firms with a Z score less than −10. Although these firms could be dropped from the analysis, it will be interesting to see in which direction they move.

The bankrupt sample had a mean Z score of −7.99 and a standard deviation of .03337927, the nonbankrupt sample a mean Z score of 9.18 and a standard deviation of .0230832, and the TDR sample a mean Z score of −.3322 and a standard deviation of 19.961155.

Figure 3

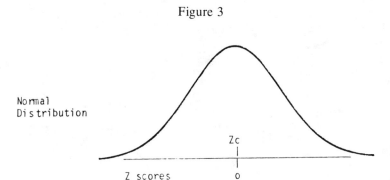

Figure 4 illustrates the results of Z scores for the TDR sample for three years prior to TDR and two years after TDR. In this scale, $\overline{Z}-$ is the average for all firms classified as bankrupt each year while $\overline{Z}+$ is the average for all firms classified as nonbankrupt each year. Zc is the cutoff point; firms above Zc are considered nonbankrupt and firms below Zc are considered bankrupt. Finally, $\overline{Z}$ is the average Z score for all firms in the TDR sample for each year.

It is interesting to note that, prior to TDR, average Z scores $(\overline{Z})$ increase slightly. However, at the inception of TDR and one year after TDR, $\overline{Z}$ decreases. Strangely, two years after TDR, $\overline{Z}$ increases to 8.64. No generalizations can be made here for two reasons. First, $\overline{Z}$ is an average, so it can be influenced by a very high or very low Z score. Second, several firms were lost after TDR, since no data were available.

A few items should be noted here. First, the mean Z score is far different from the mean Z scores of either the bankrupt or nonbankrupt samples. Next, the large standard deviation of the TDR sample is due to its bimodal distribution, part classifying as bankrupt and part as nonbankrupt. If this sample is divided into two categories, one with positive Z scores and one with negative Z scores, then the mean Z scores for each group would be more similar to the bankrupt and nonbankrupt samples, as noted above. Also, the standard deviations for each Z score group would be much smaller.

It becomes apparent that some of the firms in the TDR sample are following through the failure process. However, it is uncertain whether or not the firms classifying as nonbankrupt are, in fact, following through the failure process. There are two possible explanations. First, these firms may not be headed toward failure before the TDR event. They may be normal, healthy firms which are merely experiencing a cash flow problem at a particular point in time. There is evidence that 13 of the TDR firms may be in that position. These firms were analyzed in chapter 4. In this case, their creditors would probably have no objection to a TDR, since they would feel certain that the firm would continue as a going concern. Second, the prediction model may not be able to classify these firms accurately, since the

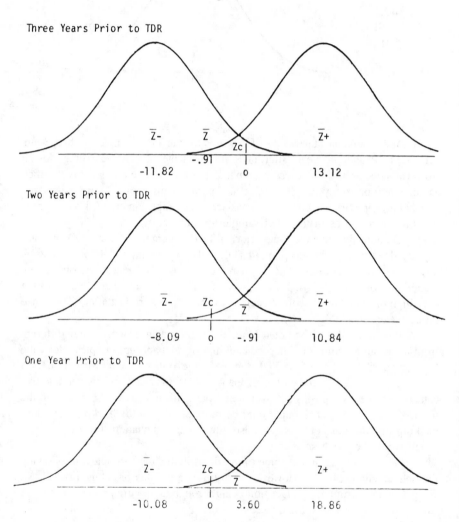

Figure 4

Figure 4 (continued)

One Year After TDR

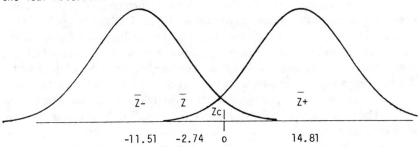

Two Years After TDR

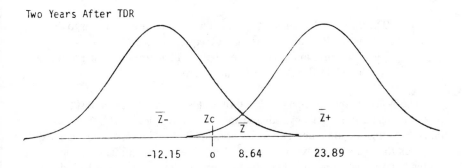

TDR date may come long before failure. For several years prior to failure, bank-ruptcy prediction models lose accuracy. So even though these firms may in fact be heading toward the failure process at this point, the model might not be able to identify them. It appears that both of these situations exist in the TDR sample. Most of these firms had declining Z scores prior to TDR; very few had constant or increasing scores, which would indicate health.

Since the Z scores did not lie in a normal distribution, non-parametric statistical testing is appropriate. Using non-parametric statistical tests may be open to criticism because the Z scores were computed using multiple discriminant analysis, a parametric statistical technique. However, first, to date, there have been no non-parametric procedures developed which perform the functions of MDA. Second, as was mentioned in the limitations section of chapter 1, MDA has proven to be a powerful technique even when the assumption of normality is relaxed. It has also been used successfully in other bankruptcy studies (Altman, 1977; Rose and Giroux, 1980). However, non-parametric statistical techniques will be used for further testing of the Z score results because the distribution is not normal. The reason for choos-ing non-parametric tests over parametric tests is that their results are more conser-vative. The bimodal distribution was more severe in MDA than with the non-parametric tests.

The first hypothesis to be tested is intended to determine if the changes in Z scores approaching the TDR date are moving in the bankrupt direction. The hypothesis to be tested is as follows:

HO: The difference in mean Z scores before TDR from one year to the next for the TDR firms is less than or equal to zero.

H1:   The difference in mean Z scores before TDR from one year to the next for the TDR firms is greater than zero.

The Wilcoxin matched-pairs, signed-ranks test was used here to test two years of Z scores at a time. This hypothesis was tested three times. The first test com-pared Z scores for three and two years prior to TDR. The second test compared Z scores for two and one year prior to TDR. Finally, the third test compared Z scores for one year prior to TDR and the year of TDR. If the null hypothesis is false, then it can be concluded that the firms' Z scores are decreasing from year to year approaching the TDR date.

Using the large sample approximation for these tests, the results shown in the following table were obtained. At two years and one year prior to TDR, the mean Z scores are worsening for the firms at the 95 percent confidence level. For three years prior to TDR, no conclusions can be drawn. There is therefore some indica-tion that the firms' financial positions were getting worse as they approached their TDRs.

Since, on the average, Z scores are worsening two years and one year prior to TDR, something can be said about the TDR firms in general. Since the variables

Time Period	Test Statistic
	Z
Three and two years prior to TDR	2.09
Two and one years prior to TDR	-4.15*
One year prior and year of TDR	-3.99*

*significant at the .05 α level

are heavily based on income and debt, it could be assumed that either the TDR firms' income was worsening or their losses were getting larger. This, in fact, was the case for most firms prior to TDR. Long-term debt soared during this period while more and more firms experienced net losses in these years.

The next hypothesis to be tested determines what direction the Z scores take after TDR. The following hypothesis was tested:

HO: The difference in mean Z scores after TDR from one year to the next for the TDR firms is zero.

H1: The difference in mean Z scores after TDR from one year to the next for the TDR firms is not zero.

The same Wilcoxin matched-pairs, signed-ranks test was used here, but in this case the two-sided hypothesis was appropriate, since it was not known in which direction the firms' Z scores would go. This hypothesis was also tested three times. For one year after TDR, the large sample approximation formula was used, while for two and three years after TDR, the t statistic for this test was computed, since the data available in these years diminished. The following table shows the results.

Time Period	Test	Statistic
	Z	T
Year of TDR and one year after TDR	-.56	
One and two years after TDR		57
Two and three years after TDR		3

As the table shows, none of these test statistics was found to be significant. The firms' individual ratios did not change to any great extent from year to year. Rejection of the null hypothesis would have indicated that mean Z scores were significantly changing for years after TDR, but the null hypothesis cannot be rejected in any of the cases. Therefore it cannot be concluded at the 95 percent confidence level that the firms' mean Z scores or financial positions changed significantly after TDR.

Although there were no significant results here, a few things can be noticed. In the first year after TDR, the Z score of $-.56$ indicates that on average the Z scores continued to decrease, but not significantly. The confidence level here is only 57.54 percent. The t score for two years after TDR indicates that Z scores increased, but below the 89.6 percent confidence level. Finally, in the third year after TDR, the t score indicates rising Z scores above the 92.2 percent confidence level but below the 96.9 percent confidence level.

For two year prior to TDR, the firms' financial positions were weakening as their Z scores decreased. During the first year after TDR, Z scores still decreased, but not significantly. At that point, then, the firms appeared to be stabilizing, that is, getting neither worse nor better. For two and three years after TDR, Z scores improved, but again not significantly, but at least the firms were no worse off after TDR than before TDR.

In the firms' financial statements after TDR, there was a general upward trend for income of 66.67 percent. Some firms still experienced net losses in these years, but usually smaller net losses than they suffered prior to TDR.

Long-term debt was reduced for most firms after TDR as a result of the debt restructuring. However, in many cases the current portion of long-term debt rose. In these cases, the restructuring terms called for reduced principal but a substantial amount currently due. This might explain why the Z scores did not increase significantly.

The third hypothesis tested tries to determine the same results as before, but in a slightly different manner. The McNemar test for related samples will be used. This test uses the results of the Z scores and will determine if a significant number of firms changed their bankrupt or nonbankrupt status for three years prior to and three years after TDR.

The following hypothesis was tested:

$$H0: \quad p1 = p2 \text{ or } p1 - p2 = 0$$
$$H1: \quad p1 \neq p2 \text{ or } p1 - p2 \neq 0$$

where $p1$ is the proportion of TDR firms classified as bankrupt in one year and $p2$ is the proportion of TDR firms classified as bankrupt in the next year.

A two-by-two matrix can be formed as shown in the following table.

		Time Period 2		
		Bankrupt	Nonbankrupt	Total
Time	Bankrupt	A	B	A&B
Period 1	Nonbankrupt	C	D	C&D
	Total	A&C	B&D	N

By using a sequence of two time periods, the table can be set up as follows:

A = Firms which classified as bankrupt in periods one and two
B = Firms which classified as bankrupt in period one and nonbankrupt in period two
C = Firms which classified as nonbankrupt in periods one and two
D = Firms which classified as nonbankrupt in period one and bankrupt in period two

Instead of measuring for differences in mean Z scores, changes in the frequencies of classification will be measured. Each one-year time period was tested between three years prior to TDR and three years after TDR. The results shown in the following table were obtained.

Time Period	Test Statistic
	Z
three and two years prior to TDR	2.50*
two and one year prior to TDR	-1.15
one year prior and year of TDR	- .77
year of TDR and one year after TDR	0.00
one and two years after TDR	
two and three years after TDR	

*significant at the .05 α level

The first time period tested produced an unexpected result. A significant number of firms at the 95 percent confidence level changed their bankrupt-nonbankrupt status. This result is strange, because the shift was from bankrupt to nonbankrupt, not from nonbankrupt to bankrupt as might have been expected. For several years prior to TDR, most of the TDR firms experienced sporadic net losses. One year they would report profits while in the next they would report losses. The further back one goes prior to TDR, the more inconsistent the trends appear. Although this indicates instability, it may also explain the shift in the opposite direction. Perhaps three years prior to TDR is too far off to analyze these firms with a bankruptcy model, in which case, the descriptive analysis in chapter 4 may be more reliable.

The descriptive data analyzed comprised EBIT, RE, TC, EBIT/INT, WC/TA, CLTD/TA, and LTD/TL. For most of these items the nonbankrupt firms had the strongest results while the bankrupt firms had the weakest results. However, the most important item was WC/TA since the TDR sample had negative WC/TA while for the other two samples it was positive. This result indicates a severe funds flow problem for the TDR firms.

The results of the next two time periods were not unexpected. There is a shift toward bankruptcy status, but not a significant one. The Z score shifts were significant for these periods, but evidently not large enough to cause the firms' bankrupt-nonbankrupt status to change significantly. The Z statistic of 0.00 for the first year after TDR indicates that the number of shifts to nonbankrupt status was equal to the number away from it, so overall there was no significant change in the firms' financial positions in one direction or the other in the first year after TDR.

According to the raw data for this period, most firms' income and working capital increased, but not to a great extent. An explanation could be that not enough time had passed for the TDR firms to strengthen their financial positions. Analysis of these firms several years into the future will ultimately show whether or not TDR has been successful.

In chapter 4, specific attention was given to working capital (WC) and earnings before interest and taxes (EBIT). A general trend of decreasing WC before TDR and increasing WC after TDR was found. This indicates that the TDR firms' funds flow problem was worsening prior to TDR, but after TDR the funds flow problem began to improve. Working capital appears to be the most critical factor in the study of TDR firms. EBIT for most firms was negative or sporadic before TDR, but it was higher than for the bankrupt firms on average. This result is consistent with the failure process. The TDR firms' losses were not yet as severe as those of the bankrupt firms.

The last two time periods could not be tested. To implement the McNemar test, the total number of status shifts has to be at least 10. For two and three years after TDR, the number of shifts in classification was less than 10. Therefore, no conclusions can be drawn for these time periods.

The next hypothesis to be tested attempts to determine whether a significant number of firms fall into either the bankrupt or nonbankrupt categories. This test is carried out for each year from three years prior to TDR to three years after TDR. Rejection of the null hypothesis leads to the conclusion that the Z scores fall into either the bankrupt or nonbankrupt category. From the classification results shown in table 7, it appears that the null hypothesis is not rejected, because of the bimodal distribution.

The following hypothesis was tested:

$$H0: \quad M = M0$$
$$H1: \quad M \neq M0$$

In this hypothesis, M is the Z mean score computed for each firm, while M0 is the median of Z scores. The results are shown in the following table.

Time Period	Test Statistic
	T
three years prior to TDR	- .67
two years prior to TDR	-1.32
one year prior to TDR	0.00
year of TDR	- .91
one year after TDR	- .92
two years after TDR	-1.20
three years after TDR	- .50

As was expected, there were no significant results for any year under analysis. Therefore, it cannot be concluded that a significant number of firms classified as either bankrupt or nonbankrupt at any time. This result supports the bimodal distribution discussed earlier.

The final hypothesis tests whether the TDR population is homogeneous with respect to the bankrupt and/or nonbankrupt populations used to derive the discriminant model. The chi-square test for homogeneity can achieve this result. The hypothesis to be tested may be stated as follows:

H0:   The sampled populations of TDR firms are homogeneous.

H1:   The sampled populations of TDR firms are not homogeneous.

Rejection of the null hypothesis leads to the conclusion that a dichotomy exists between the TDR and the bankrupt sample or the TDR and the nonbankrupt sample based on each of the samples' classification results. Again, each year is tested from three years prior to TDR to three years after TDR.

A two-by-two contingency table can be formed as shown in table 8.

For each year prior to TDR, the actual results will be used for the bankrupt and nonbankrupt firms as shown in table 6. For the year of TDR and subsequent years, the results used for the MDA model (one year prior to bankruptcy) will be used. These results are shown in table 5 (p. 65). For the TDR sample, actual results will be used for each year, as shown in table 7 (p. 69).

Table 8
Chi-Square Contingency Table

1.

	Bankrupt	Nonbankrupt	Total
TDR Sample			
Non Bankrupt			
Total			

2.

	Bankrupt	Nonbankrupt	Total
TDR Sample			
Bankrupt Sample			
Total			

The results of the chi-square test for homogeneity are as shown in the following table.

	Nonbankrupt Sample	Bankrupt Sample
Time period	Test Statistic x^2	Test Statistic x^2
three years prior to TDR	4.9900*	.1587
two years prior to TDR	2.1276	5.2372*
one year prior to TDR	.0713	.3882
year of TDR	21.7204*	10.8308*
one year after TDR	21.0511*	9.6469*
two years after TDR	8.7169*	18.3685*
three years after TDR	9.3677*	9.9901*

*significant at the .05 α level

For three years prior to TDR, a dichotomy existed between the TDR and non-bankrupt samples, indicating that the TDR sample and the nonbankrupt sample were not homogeneous. For two years prior to TDR, a dichotomy existed between the TDR and bankrupt samples, while for one year prior to TDR, no dichotomies existed. There is no indication here, then, that the TDR sample was significantly different from either the bankrupt or nonbankrupt sample for each year prior to TDR.

Four explanations can be offered here. One possible explanation for these conflicting results is that these firms actually changed their financial positions in the given directions each year. Another explanation might be that the farther the time period analyzed is from the TDR date, the less reliable become the MDA function and the Z scores. Third, there may exist more than two discrete groups in the MDA model. If this is the case, the Z scores computed would be less reliable, resulting in inconsistent findings. Finally, if prior to TDR the firms were implementing accounting changes to mask their financial positions, then the computed Z scores would be based on these masked financial data.

There is evidence to suppose that the TDR sample may, in fact, be distinct and separate from both the bankrupt and nonbankrupt samples. A discriminant function computed using three groups should result in Z scores clustering around three points instead of two. If the TDR sample had Z scores which clustered around its own point, then that would also support this explanation. This could also explain the bimodal distribution of Z scores computed earlier for the TDR firms.

Again, from the raw data prior to TDR, it was previously observed that reported income and losses were erratic over time. Since the discriminant function was largely based on income factors, the erratic behavior of the firms could, in fact, cause this shift in homogeneity. Again, it is possible that three years prior to TDR is too distant from the bankruptcy event to be evaluated properly by a bankruptcy prediction model. Finally, the results may be due to the fact that the TDR firms follow a bimodal distribution. The positive and negative Z scores combined together may affect the results.

The results for the year of TDR and subsequent years are more meaningful. In each of these years, a dichotomous relationship existed between the TDR and bankrupt samples and also between the TDR and nonbankrupt samples, which is consistent with the bimodal distribution obtained. The homogeneous relationships observed in years prior to TDR resulted because of the bankrupt and nonbankrupt data used. The classification results for the TDR sample were based on the MDA function for one year prior to bankruptcy. Therefore, there is an indication that the TDR sample had classification results similar to the bankrupt and nonbankrupt samples. This is evident in the periods where the homogeneous relationships occurred.

After TDR, nine of the firms filed for bankruptcy under the National Bankruptcy Act. Several of them still continued to operate as of 1982. This result provides evidence that in some cases, a TDR may be successful. If a firm can implement a successful TDR, it may be able to remove itself from the failure process. Only a few firms have actually gone out of existence, and only three have merged with other firms. So even though the TDR itself failed in a few cases, these firms appear to be following through the failure process. They have taken the next available course of action.

Summary

An MDA model was computed using MULDIS. The model computed was a 12-variable linear function derived from the bankrupt and nonbankrupt samples. The TDR firms were then analyzed using this model from three years prior to TDR up through three years after TDR.

Next, several non-parametric statistical tests were performed to determine any similarities or dissimilarities between the TDR sample and the bankrupt and non-bankrupt samples. These tests were also designed to determine whether the TDR firms' financial positions were worsening or improving prior to TDR and after TDR.

In summary, these statistical tests indicated that the TDR firms became financially weaker approaching the TDR date, based on their respective Z scores. After the TDR date, there was no indication that the firms turned around and became healthy, but there was also no indication that the firms worsened further after TDR. At most then, they may have stabilized for up to three years after TDR. As has been mentioned earlier, analysis of future years will ultimately demonstrate the success or failure of the TDR.

The descriptive analysis presented in chapter 4 provided stronger evidence that the TDR firms were becoming financially worse off prior to TDR based on earnings and working capital. After TDR, descriptive analysis indicated that the firms did begin to improve.

6

Conclusions

For several years, firms have been entering into troubled debt restructurings with their creditors. These TDRs are informal agreements between debtor and creditor firms. Because no financial reporting requirements existed prior to 1977, most firms did not disclose their TDRs in their financial statements. Therefore, data were virtually impossible to obtain in order to perform empirical research. Today, with several years of data available, empirical studies in the area have become possible.

In past studies, TDRs have been tied to the failure process. Before a firm faces bankruptcy and/or liquidation, it may experience operating results below expectations, inability to pay dividends, net losses and negative cash flow trends, lowered bond ratings, and deteriorating results year after year. Finally, the firm may face loan default. A viable alternative may be a TDR, to help the firm avoid bankruptcy with the approval of its creditors. If successful, the TDR may help the firm to turn around and become profitable again.

Two very important questions that have never been addressed up to this point are as follows: Do firms that restructure their debt possess characteristics of bankrupt firms prior to restructuring? And do these firms, after restructuring, manage in fact to turn themselves around and become profitable concerns again? This study sought to answer these questions.

In the past, several bankruptcy prediction models have been developed. The most common predictor variables used have been financial ratios. In this study, another bankruptcy prediction model was developed also using financial ratios as predictor variables. Variables were computed using the same financial statement items that Altman (1977) used. Multiple discriminant analysis was used to develop the model, since it is the technique which has had the best classification accuracy thus far (Hamer, 1982). Finally, a sample of TDR firms was analyzed using the bankruptcy prediction model.

Summary of Results

Three samples of firms were obtained for analysis. First, a sample of bankrupt firms was constructed covering a 10-year period. These firms were all listed on the COMPUSTAT Industrial Research File, which makes data easy to obtain. Next, a sample of nonbankrupt firms was matched by industry type and size with the bankrupt sample. These firms were all listed on the COMPUSTAT Industrial File as well. Finally, a sample of TDR firms was obtained by DISCLOSURE, Inc. These firms disclosed TDRs in their 1981 financial statements. DISCLOSURE selects all of the firms reporting a specific item in their latest financial statements. The procedure does not go back to past financial statements; however, the firms must report a TDR each year while it exists, so many of the TDRs reported in this study began prior to 1981.

First, the TDR firms were analyzed descriptively. A summary of the types of TDRs implemented was presented, as well as a history of two of the TDR firms, one which came out of its troubled position and one which subsequently filed for bankruptcy. Possible reasons for these firms' positions after the TDR were suggested.

In examining the types of TDRs, it was found that most firms either implemented a reduction in principal or issued common or preferred stock in settlement of debt. Fewer firms extended maturity dates, lowered interest rates, or reduced accrued interest.

The characteristics of TDR firms were presented and discussed. It was found that 78.33 percent of the TDR firms experienced negative EBIT in at least one year prior to TDR, indicating financial difficulties. Prior to TDR, 77.33 percent of the TDR firms had a deficit in retained earnings, which may indicate net losses year after year. Finally, 36.67 percent of the firms had deficit capital balances. These findings indicate that the majority of these firms were having financial difficulties prior to TDR.

The results of the analysis of four financial ratios for the bankrupt, nonbankrupt, and TDR samples were as expected except for WC/TA (working capital/total assets). WC/TA was found to be lowest for the TDR firms. Also, WC/TA on average was found to be negative for the TDR firms. This result provides strong evidence that these firms were experiencing cash flow problems which made it impossible for them to make payments on their debt. Further analysis of working capital and other funds flow measures is needed. This critical factor has been previously emphasized and may prove to be a key factor in the study of TDR firms.

For the other ratios analyzed, the nonbankrupt firms had results which indicated that they were in the strongest financial position. The bankrupt sample results indicated that these firms were in the financially worst position. The TDR firms were stronger than the bankrupt firms and weaker than the nonbankrupt firms.

The following observations were made:

1. The TDR firms, overall, were experiencing negative EBIT, some of them year after year.
2. The TDR firms reported interest expense very close to the bankrupt sample.

3. Prior to TDR, most of the firms had negative and decreasing WC.
4. After TDR, most of the firms had positive and increasing WC.
5. Thirteen firms never showed negative EBIT and did not deteriorate prior to TDR.

Next, using the samples of bankrupt and nonbankrupt firms, an MDA bankruptcy model was developed and a 12-variable linear model was derived using financial ratios. The ratios selected for analysis were those found to have predictive power in previous studies. The MULDIS package used forward stepwise selection procedures in order to eliminate any ratios found to be unpredictive.

Once the MDA model was developed, it was used to analyze TDR firms. Data for the TDR firms were obtained from the firms' 10-K reports and Z scores were computed for each firm in the sample. The period of analysis was from three years prior to the TDR date through three years after the TDR date.

It was found that prior to TDR, only half of the firms classified as bankrupt, resulting in a bimodal distribution. The question of why the majority of these firms did not classify as bankrupt before TDR remains unanswered, but three possible reasons can be offered. First, prior to TDR, income among the firms was erratic over time, and it may be because of this that, although the firms were not doing well in general prior to TDR, the MDA model did not classify them as bankrupt.

Another possible explanation is that the MDA model was either too conservative or was not able to discriminate TDR firms well. This leads to the third explanation. There may exist three discrete groups for the discriminant function. The TDR sample may be separate and distinct from the bankrupt and nonbankrupt groups. This would also explain the bimodal distribution. There is evidence to support this third explanation, since working capital was significantly different for the TDR firms and the other two groups. Some measure of funds flow may be the critical variable to distinguish the TDR sample from the other two.

Next, through non-parametric statistical testing, it was found that for one and two years prior to TDR, the firms' Z scores declined, indicating weakening financial positions. However, the decline was not significant enough to change the bankrupt-nonbankrupt status of the TDR firms classifying as nonbankrupt. During the first year following the TDR, the Z scores continued to decline, but not significantly so. Again, it cannot be concluded that these firms' financial positions were weakening.

For two and three years following the TDR, the firms' Z scores improved somewhat, but not significantly so. None of these changes occurring after the TDR were strong enough to cause a shift in the bankrupt-nonbankrupt status of the firms classifying as bankrupt.

One conclusion that can be drawn here is that since the firms' Z scores worsened prior to TDR, their financial positions were weakening. After TDR, since the Z scores did not change significantly, the financial positions of the TDR firms had stabilized. Although there is no indication that these firms turned themselves around as a result of the TDR, at least they seem to have held their positions at a stable level. From observation of the raw data, it could be seen that the firms' liquidity, operating, and debt ratios seemed to improve slightly after TDR, but not significantly so. An extension of the current study into future periods may find these firms strengthening to a greater degree.

Finally, it was found that for all years following the TDR a dichotomy existed between the TDR and bankrupt firms and also between the TDR and nonbankrupt firms. Therefore it may be concluded that after TDR, the TDR firms are not homogeneous with either the bankrupt or nonbankrupt firms with respect to their classification results.

There are two possible explanations for this result. First, the TDR firms, after TDR, may still be somewhere between the bankrupt and nonbankrupt firms on the bankruptcy continuum. Second, as was mentioned earlier, it is possible that there are more than two discrete groups in the MDA model. There are possibly three groups that are distinguishable—bankrupt, nonbankrupt, and TDR firms. If this is true, the TDR firms would not be homogeneous with either of the two other samples.

The detailed analysis concerned the JFLF Company, an established furniture company which has suffered from losses in the past few years, and the Lexicon Corporation, a newly formed computer company. The JFLF Company restructured its debt by extending its maturity date while the Lexicon Corporation reduced its principal twice. The JFLF Company filed for bankruptcy subsequent to its TDR.

Three possible explanations are offered for the JFLF Company's unsuccessful TDR. First, the TDR may have come too late. Second, the terms of the TDR may have been too strict. A reduction in principal might have been better. Third, the company may have been fundamentally in such a financially bad position that nothing could have helped it avoid the failure process and bankruptcy.

The Lexicon Corporation continues to operate. Even though it is still incurring losses each year, the losses have been substantially reduced. Because the bank allowed the company to reduce its principal twice, it must have believed that this young growth company had a marketable product which would soon make the firm profitable. As of 1982, it appeared that the TDR helped put the Lexicon Corporation on the right track. It is hoped that future research can address these topics in more detail.

Conclusions from the Descriptive Study

It can be concluded from the descriptive analysis that all but 13 firms entered the failure process prior to TDR, experiencing operating results below expectations, net loss and negative funds flow trends, and deteriorating results year after year. After TDR, there appears to be a reversal in these trends for some firms, but complete data were not available to make overall conclusions.

Thirteen of the 60 TDR firms did not appear to be following the failure process. These firms may in fact have been healthy firms with a cash or funds flow problem at a particular point in time. Only 2 of these firms implemented a reduction in principal, indicating the probability that the other 11 firms could repay their debt.

The negative WC/TA ratio observed for the TDR firms supports the conclusion that these firms had a severe funds flow problem. So even though the 13 firms appeared to be healthy, a severe cash or funds flow problem is likely to have forced them into a TDR.

From the detailed analysis it was concluded that the JFLF Company, a well-established firm, made two errors when implementing its TDR. First, the firm should have implemented a more lenient TDR such as a reduction in principal or issuance of stock. It may, of course, have had no power over this decision. The extension of maturity date did not prove to be effective. Second, it appears that by the time the JFLF Company implemented its TDR, it was already too far along the failure process to reverse itself. Perhaps wiser management would have seen the need for a TDR a few years earlier. Earlier implementation might have saved the firm.

The Lexicon Corporation, a newly formed company, has already implemented two reductions in principal. Although the company continues to operate at a loss, the amounts of these losses have been drastically reduced. This is common with many new companies. It appears, then, that the Lexicon Corporation may become profitable soon.

The firms themselves cannot be totally responsible for the results. The banks have the final say when implementing a TDR. They may make their decision on the financial position of the firm, their relationship with the firm, or the type of industry of which the firm is a part. The last factor may be important in the cases studied here. The banks could have been influenced by the fact that the JFLF Company is in the furniture industry, which has significantly weakened in the past several years, while the Lexicon Corporation is in the computer industry, which has been growing fast.

Conclusions from Statistical Testing

The statistical testing showed that for two years and one year prior to TDR, the firms' Z scores were worsening. This supports the descriptive analysis of earnings and working capital data. However, after TDR, no significant changes in Z scores were found. This means that the financial positions of the TDR firms did not change significantly. Although the approach of statistically testing Z scores may be questioned, it has been used by Altman and Brenner to test for stock market reactions (1981). They reported similar results achieved by the Efficient Markets Hypothesis research. So there is support for this analysis.

When testing for homogeneity, the results were inconsistent. One possible explanation seems to warrant the most attention. The TDR sample may be distinct from the bankrupt and nonbankrupt samples. In this case an MDA model could be computed using three groups, where the TDR group would not be homogeneous with either the bankrupt or nonbankrupt groups. The critical factor supporting this conclusion is the TDR group's negative WC/TA ratio. This is significantly different from the other groups, and could be a key discriminating factor among all three groups.

In general, it appears that the TDR firms are in financial difficulty and have started the failure process. All but 13 firms were having financial problems prior to TDR. The 13 firms, which appeared healthy, still encountered a funds flow problem. This is not an uncommon event for a healthy firm. Earnings and working capital data provide the strongest evidence for these firms' deteriorating positions. The MDA model also provides evidence of their deteriorating positions.

After TDR, there is some evidence that working capital data help to support this statement. However, statistical testing of the Z scores from the MDA model after TDR provides no conclusions.

Suggestions for Future Research

Throughout this study, mention has been made of ideas for future research. First, an extension of the current study could carry this analysis of TDR firms into future years. It may, in fact, take several years after a TDR for a firm to turn around. Along the same lines as in this study, MDA could be used to predict a TDR instead of using a bankruptcy model to analyze TDR firms. In other words, a TDR sample could be matched with a sample of firms with no TDR. Then a discriminant function could be developed in an attempt to predict TDRs.

One of the more interesting ideas for future research would be to determine if a particular type of TDR proves to be more successful than other types. There are so many factors influencing a TDR that this topic, although important, would be very difficult to pursue.

Another interesting project would be to follow these firms further into the future to see what their outcomes are. Some of them may merge or some may become bankrupt. The factors which explain why some firms can continue as going concerns while others end in bankruptcy and liquidation could be sought.

Top management of the TDR firms could be interviewed to find out how each TDR came about. It would be interesting to know how much bargaining is involved between debtor and creditor firms when implementing a TDR. Since the bank or other lender must first agree to the specific terms of a TDR, the debtor firm does not always end up with the type of TDR it might prefer.

The creditors of the TDR firms could also be interviewed to see how TDR has affected them. For example, they could be asked if they would be willing to agree to a TDR again with the same firm or another firm. A TDR's impact on its creditors might prove to be a very fruitful study. Other creditors might benefit from the results. This topic could be carried further into the banking industry.

As an extension of this study, discriminant analysis could be performed with three groups, the bankrupt, nonbankrupt, and TDR samples. Because of the interesting results found in this study using working capital data, this might prove valuable. Another important project along these lines is to analyze working capital in detail for the TDR firms. It was shown that working capital decreased before TDR and increased after TDR. An analysis of the changes in the components of working capital for these firms may provide other key factors for distinguishing and understanding TDR firms.

Another question that is important to answer is whether any specific sorts of TDR are more effective than others in aiding firms to avoid bankruptcy. A nonparametric test, the Friedman test, may test for differences between these factors. This test is the non-parametric counterpart of the analysis of variance. TDRs may consist of one or more of the following:

1. reduction of interest rate
2. extension of maturity date
3. reduction of principal
4. reduction of accrued interest
5. issuing of equity
6. transfer of receivables.

Limitations

Several limitations of this study have been discussed. First, it may be impossible to isolate a TDR so it can be analyzed by itself. This is a problem cited in many studies. However, because other factors, such as economic conditions, are common to all firms, these different factors can be eliminated to a certain extent.

There are several limitations in using MDA, which were presented in chapter 1. The variance-covariance matrices of the predictors (financial ratios) should be the same for both groups (bankrupt and nonbankrupt firms). The variables should follow a normal distribution. However, even when these requirements are violated, MDA has proven to be a powerful tool. The Z scores computed from the model have little intuitive interpretation. The matching procedures involved are also somewhat arbitrary.

Other limitations of this study are, first, that the TDR firms were not matched by industry and size to the bankrupt and nonbankrupt firms (which were matched) to determine if the TDR firms follow the failure process. As was mentioned earlier, if a TDR firm is in the failure process, its Z score should decline as it approaches the TDR date. Z scores were computed for these firms. Then, it was these Z scores which were statistically analyzed. Therefore, the Z scores are related to all three samples. However, the parameters of the MDA model were derived from the bankrupt and nonbankrupt samples. Since the non-parametric statistical tests analyzed Z scores within firms from year to year, the changes in those Z scores should be meaningful.

Since the TDR sample was not random, the possibility exists that the results are biased. However, since DISCLOSURE, Inc. is the best source available, it was used here. The bankrupt and nonbankrupt samples were also nonrandom. This problem, however, has been cited as common in the literature and is not considered detrimental to the results (Eisenbeis and Avery, 1972).

Finally, with regard to the non-parametric statistical tests, the importance of the Z scores of the TDR firms may have been overemphasized. However, for each test performed, the raw data for the firms were examined in order to support or dispute the conclusions of the statistical tests. In all cases, the conclusions from the statistical testing could be supported. The analysis of the raw data indicated that the TDR firms were weakening prior to TDR.

There are other limitations deriving from the source of the TDR sample. It was found that DISCLOSURE, Inc. had made some errors in listing the TDR firms. Eight firms listed by DISCLOSURE, Inc. had never implemented or disclosed a TDR. Since the process of identifying specific disclosures in financial statements requires individuals to examine these financial statements in detail, the reports are subject to human error. Although every effort was made to minimize these weaknesses, they cannot be totally eliminated. It is hoped that any weaknesses present in the study are not strong enough to significantly bias the results.

Another limitation again lies in the TDR sample. As mentioned earlier, DISCLOSURE only selected firms which reported a TDR in their 1981 financial statements. In some cases, the TDR went back several years and still existed. However, in many cases, the TDR was at most one year old. Some of the older TDRs may have been settled, or some of these firms may have gone out of existence.

Finally, because many of the TDRs are current, the analysis of TDR firms involves a period of five years. However, the MDA model was developed using a ten-year period to obtain an acceptable sample size. Although this may have no effect on the results, there still exists the possibility of a bias.

Appendix A

Samples

33.	Lloyd S. Electronics	81
34.	Love Oil Co., Inc.	80
35.	Mayfair Supermarkets	81
36.	Medco Jewelry Corp.	80
37.	Mego International	80
38.	Morton Shoe Co., Inc.	81
39.	NCC Industries, Inc.	77
40.	North American Biologicals, Inc.	81
41.	Pacesetter Industries	79,82
42.	Pantry Pride	81
43.	Pathcom, Inc.	78
44.	Pfizer, Inc.	81
45.	Quality Care	82
46.	REM Metals Corp.	81
47.	Russell, Burdsall, & Ward	80
48.	Safeguard Business Systems	80
49.	Scan Data Corp.	80
50.	Scanfax Systems	77,78
51.	Sea Pines iCo.	78
52.	Superscope Inc.	80
53.	Tiffany Industries	78,81
54.	Topps & Trowsers	81
55.	Twin Fair Inc.	82
56.	Universal Container	79
57.	Wells Benrus Corp.	79
58.	White Motor Corp.	79
59.	Willcox & Gibbs, Inc.	80
60.	Xonics, Inc.	81

B.	Bankrupt Firms	Year of Bankruptcy
1.	Electronic Computer Programming Inst. Inc.	75
2.	General Alloys Co.	73
3.	TMA Company	73
4.	Westates Petroleum Co.	76
5.	Gray Manufacturing Co.	75
6.	National Bellas Hess, Inc.	74
7.	DCA Development Corp.	73
8.	Electrospace	74
9.	American Book-Stratford Press	73
10.	Potter Instrument Co., Inc.	75
11.	American Recreation Group,	73
12.	Harvard Industries, Inc.	73
13.	Waltham Industries Corp.	72
14.	Botany Industries	72
15.	Mammoth Mart, Inc.	74
16.	Arlan's Dept. Stores, Inc.	74
17.	Bohack Corp.	77
18.	Penn Fruit Co., Inc.	75
19.	W.T. Grant Co.	75
20.	Allied Artists Industries, Inc.	79
21.	Allied Supermarkets, Inc.	78
22.	Combustion Equipment Assoc. Inc.	80

23.	FDI Inc.	78
24.	Garland Corp.	80
25.	Lynnwear Corp.	81
26.	Mansfield Tire & Rubber Co.	79
27.	Metropolitan Greetings, Inc.	79
28.	Penn Dixie Industries, Inc.	80
29.	Piedmont Industries, Inc.	79
30.	Poloron Products, Inc.	81
31.	Richton International Corp.	80
32.	Vendo Co.	77
33.	West Chemical Prod., Inc.	79
34.	Whippany Paper Board Co.	80
35.	Spatrain Lines, Inc.	81

C. Nonbankrupt Firms

AAR Corporation

Shaer Shoe Corp.
Fluke Manufacturing, Inc.
Cooper Laboratories
Keystone Industries
Pittsburgh Brewing Co.
Coleco Industries, Inc.
Global Marine, Inc.
Ennis Business Forms, Inc.

Altec Corp.
HMW Industries, Inc.
Altamil Corp.
Interphoto, Inc.
Russ Togs, Inc.
Caldor, Inc.
Dillard's Dept. Stores Inc
Alterman Foods, Inc.
Foodarama Supermarkets
Gamble-Skogmo, Inc.
Riblet Products Corp.

National Tea Co.
Twin Disc Inc.

Tokheim Corp.
Barco of CA
Barco of CA
Mohawk Rubber Co.
Williamhouse Regency Inc.
Ceco Corp.
Barco of CA
Oakwood Homes
Swank, Inc.
Wurlitzer Co.
Oakite Prod.
American Israeli Paper
Mills
Moore McCormack
Resources, Inc.

Appendix B

Ratios Used in Analysis

		Percentage of Discriminating Power Accounted for by Each Variable
1.	Working capital/total assets*	10.07343%
2.	Retained earnings/total assets	
3.	Income before extraordinary items /total assets*	3.322073%
4.	Earnings before interest and taxes/total assets*	.3233316%
5.	Book value of equity/book value of debt	
6.	Earnings before interest and taxes/interest expense*	4.523617%
7.	Current assets/current liabilities	
8.	Common equity/total capital	
9.	Current assets/total assets*	7.076948%
10.	Current liabilities/total assets*	.2482795%
11.	Earnings before taxes/total assets*	1.964262%
12.	Long-term debt/total assets	
13.	Current long-term debt/total assets*	5.217768%
14.	Current long-term debt/current assets*	6.265601%
15.	Current long-term debt/current liabilities	
16.	Current long-term debt/total capital	
17.	Current long-term debt/common equity	
18.	Long-term debt/total capital*	16.36950%
19.	Long-term debt/common equity*	27.074255%
20.	Long-term debt/total liabilities*	17.54093%
21.	Total assets/total liabilities	
22.	Total liabilities/total capital	

23. Interest expense/total liabilities
24. Common equity/total liabilities
25. Interest expense/earnings before
interest and taxes

99.99999%**

*found to be significant by Muldis
**rounding error

Appendix C

Types of Restructuring

	Number of Firms	Number of Firms Using One Type of Restructuring
Reduction In Principal	25	12
Issuance Of Common Stock	13	5
Issuance Of Preferred Stock	11	6
Extension Of Of Maturity Date	17	5
Reduction In Interest Rate	5	1
Reduction In Accrued Interest	6	2

Combination Of Terms

	Type	Number of Firms
Reduction In Principal +	Issuance Of Common Stock	3
Reduction In Principal +	Extension Of Maturity Date	4
Reduction In Principal +	Reduction In Accrued Interest	1

Reduction In Principal	+	Issuance Of Common Stock	+	Extension Of Maturity Date		1
Reduction In Principal	+	Issuance Of Common Stock	+	Reduction In Accrued Interest		1
Reduction In Principal	+	Issuance Of Common Stock	+	Issuance Of Preferred Stock		1
Reduction In Principal	+	Issuance Of Preferred Stock				1
Reduction In Principal	+	Extension Of Maturity Date	+	Reduction In Interest Rate		1
Issuance Of Common Stock	+	Extension Of Maturity Date				2
Issuance Of Common Stock	+	Extension Of Maturity Date	+	Reduction In Accrued Interest		1
Issuance Of Preferred Stock	+	Extension Of Maturity Date	+	Reduction In Interest Rate		1
Issuance Of Preferred Stock	+	Extension Of Maturity Date	+	Reduction In Interest Rate	+ Reduction In Accrued Interest	1
Extension Of Maturity Rate	+	Reduction In Interest Rate				1

References

Altman, Edward I. "Financial Ratios, Discriminant Analysis and the Prediction of Corporate Bankruptcy." *The Journal of Finance* (September 1968), pp. 589–609.

———. "Corporate Bankruptcy Potential, Stockholder Returns and Share Valuation." *The Journal of Finance* (December 1969), pp. 887–900.

———. "Predicting Railroad Bankruptcies in America." *Bell Journal of Economics and Management Science* (Spring 1973), pp. 184–211.

———. "Capitalization of Leases and Predictability of Financial Results: A Comment." *The Accounting Review* (April 1976), pp. 408–12.

———. "Predicting Performance in the Savings and Loan Association." *Journal of Monetary Economics* (1977), pp. 443–46.

Altman, Edward I., and Brenner, M. "Information Effects and Stock Market Response to Signs of Firm Deterioration." *Journal of Financial and Quantitative Analysis* (March 1981), pp. 33–51.

Altman, Edward I., and Eisenbeis, Robert A. "Financial Application of Discriminant Analysis: A Clarification." *Journal of Financial and Quantitative Analysis* (March 1978), pp. 185–95.

Altman, Edward I., Haldeman, Robert G., and Narayanan, P. "Zeta Analysis." *The Journal of Banking and Finance* (Spring 1977), pp. 29–54.

Altman, E.I., and Joris, B. "A Financial Early Warning System for Over-the-Counter Broker-Dealers." *Journal of Finance* (September 1976), pp. 1201–17.

Altman, E.I., and McGough, T.P. "Evaluation of a Company as a Going Concern." *Journal of Accountancy* (December 1974), pp. 50–57.

Amick, Daniel, and Herbert J. Wallberg, eds. *Introductory Multivariate Analysis*. Berkeley: McCutchan Publishing, 1975.

Argenti, John. *Corporate Collapse: The Causes and Symptoms*. New York: Halsted Press, 1976.

Bankruptcy Act, Rules and Forms. St. Paul: West Publishing Co., 1978.

Baxter, N.D. "Leverage, Risk of Ruin and the Cost of Capital." *Journal of Finance* (September 1967), pp. 395–404.

Beaver, W.H. "Financial Ratios as Predictors of Failure." *Empirical Research in Accounting: Selected Studies* (1966), pp. 71–102.

———. "Alternative Accounting Measures as Predictors of Failure." *The Accounting Review* (January 1968), pp. 113–22.

———. "Market Prices, Financial Ratios, and the Prediction of Failure." *Journal of Accounting Research* (Autumn 1968), pp. 179–92.

Benishay, Haskel. "Discussion of a Prediction of Business Failure Using Accounting Data." *Empirical Research in Accounting: Selected Studies* (1973), pp. 180–82.

Beresford, Dennis R., and Groves, Ray S. "The FASB Is Active at Year End." *Financial Executive* (January 1977), pp. 10–11.

Beresford, Dennis R., and Neary, Robert D. "Accounting Approach to Troubled Debt Restructurings Advocated by FASB." *Financial Executive* (March 1977), p. 6.

_____. "FASB Says No Gain or Loss in Most Debt Restructurings." *Financial Executive* (August 1977), p. 12.

Blum, M. "Failing Company Discriminant Analysis." *Journal of Accounting Research* (Spring 1974), pp. 1–25.

Bolch, Ben W., and Huang, C.J. *Multivariate Statistical Methods for Business and Economics.* Englewood Cliffs, NJ: Prentice-Hall, 1974.

Bulow, Jeremy I., and Shoven, John B. "The Bankruptcy Decision." *The Bell Journal of Economics* (Autumn 1978), pp. 437–56.

Casey, Cornelius J., Jr. "Variation in Accounting Information Load: The Effect on Loan Officers' Predictions of Bankruptcy." *The Accounting Review* (January 1980), pp. 36–49.

Collins, Robert A. "Empirical Comparison of Bankruptcy Prediction Models." *Financial Management* (Summer 1980), pp. 52–57.

Collins, Robert A., and Green, Richard D. "Statistical Methods for Bankruptcy Forecasting." Unpublished working paper, Giannini Foundation, University of California, Davis, 1980.

Dambolena, Ismael G., and Khoury, Sarkis J. "Ratio Stability and Corporate Failure." *Journal of Finance* (September 1980), pp. 1017–26.

Daniel, Wayne W. *Applied Nonparametric Statistics.* Boston: Houghton Mifflin, 1978.

Deakin, E.B. "A Discriminant Analysis of Predictors of Business Failure." *Journal of Accounting Research* (Spring 1972), pp. 167–79.

Economic Statistics Bureau of Washington, D.C. *The Handbook of Basic Economic Statistics.* 1983.

Edmister, R.O. "An Empirical Test of Financial Ratio Analysis for Small Business Failure Prediction." *Journal of Financial and Quantitative Analysis* (March 1979), pp. 1477–93.

Eisenbeis, Robert A. "Pitfalls in the Application of Discriminant Analysis in Business, Finance, and Economics." *Journal of Finance* (June 1977), pp. 875–900.

Eisenbeis, Robert A., and Avery, Robert B. *Discriminant Analysis and Classification Procedures: Theory and Applications.* Bedford, MA: D.C. Health and Co., 1972.

Elam, R. "The Effect of Lease Data on the Predictive Ability of Financial Ratios." *The Accounting Review* (January 1975), pp. 25–43.

Explanation of the 1980 Bankruptcy Tax Act. Chicago: Commerce Clearing House, 1980.

Federal Reserve Bank of New York. *Annual Report,* 1982.

Financial Accounting Standards Board. *Financial Accounting Standards.* Chicago: Commerce Clearing House, 1978.

Foster, George. *Financial Statement Analysis.* Englewood Cliffs, NJ: Prentice-Hall, 1978.

Giroux, G.A., and Wiggins, C.E. "Chapter XI and Corporate Resuscitation." *Financial Executive* (December 1983), pp. 36–41.

Gordon, M.J. "Towards a Theory of Financial Distress." *Journal of Finance* (May 1971), pp. 347–56.

Hamer, Michelle. "Variable Selection for Multivariate Failure Prediction Models." Unpublished working paper, 1982.

Hanweck, Gerald A. "Predicting Bank Failure." Research Papers in Banking and Financial Economics, Federal Reserve Board, Washington, D.C., November 1977.

Hauge, Gabriel. "Issue and Debate: The Controversy over Restructured Debt." *Journal of Accountancy* (December 1976), pp. 82–86.

Hempel, G.H. "Quantitative Borrower Characteristics Associated with Defaults on Municipal General Obligation." *Journal of Finance* (May 1973), pp. 523–30.

Higgins, R.C., and Schall, L.D. "Corporate Bankruptcy and Conglomerate Merger." *Journal of Finance* (March 1975), pp. 93–113.

Hiltner, Arthur A., and Oien, M. Burton. "Flowchart of FASB Statement No. 15." *Journal of Accountancy* (July 1978), pp. 49–51, 53.

Ho, Thomas, and Saunders, Anthony. "A Catastrophe Model of Bank Failure." *The Journal of Finance* (December 1980), pp. 1189–1207.

Johnson, C.G. "Ratio Analysis and the Prediction of Firm Failure." *Journal of Finance* (December 1970), pp. 1166–68.

Joy, O. Maurice, and Tollefson, J.O. "On the Financial Applications of Discriminant Analysis." *Journal of Financial and Quantitative Analysis* (December 1975), pp. 723–39.

_____. "Some Clarifying Comments on Discriminant Analysis." *Journal of Financial and Quantitative Analysis* (March 1978), pp. 197–200.

Kinney, William R., Jr. "Discussion of a Prediction of Business Failure Using Accounting Data." *Empirical Research in Accounting: Selected Studies* (1973), pp. 183–87.

Kolins, Wayne. "New Guidelines Issued for Troubled Debt Restructurings." *Practical Accountant* (November/December 1977), pp. 30–31.

Kraus, Alan, and Litzenberger, Robert H. "A State-Preference Model of Optimal Financial Leverage." *The Journal of Finance* (September 1973) pp. 911–22.

Lachenbruch, Peter A. *Discriminant Analysis*. New York: Hafner Press, 1975.

McCall, A.S., and Eisenbeis, R.A. "Some Effects of Affiliations among Mutual Savings and Commercial Banks." FDIC Working Paper No. 71-1, 1970.

McFadden, D. "Conditional Logit Analysis of Qualitative Choice Behavior." in *Frontiers in Econometrics*, P. Zarembka, ed. N.Y.: Academic Press, 1973.

Mensah, Yau M. "The Differential Bankruptcy Predictive Ability of Specific Price Level Adjustments: Some Empirical Evidence." *The Accounting Review* (April 1983), pp. 228–46.

Meyer, P.A., and Pifer, H.W. "Prediction of Bank Failures." *Journal of Finance* (September 1970), pp. 853–68.

Moyer, C. "Forecasting Financial Failure: A Re-Examination." *Financial Management* (Spring 1977), pp. 11–17.

Norby, William C. "Accounting for Financial Analysis." *Financial Analyst's Journal* (September/October 1976), pp. 16, 17, 76.

Norton, Curtil L. "A Comparison of General Price Level and Historical Cost Financial Statements in the Prediction of Bankruptcy: A Reply." *The Accounting Review* (July 1980), pp. 516–21.

Norton, Curtil L., and Smith, Ralph E. "A Comparison of General Price Level and Historical Cost Financial Statements in the Prediction of Bankruptcy." *The Accounting Review* (January 1979), pp. 72–87.

Ohlson, James A. "Financial Ratios and the Probabilistic Prediction of Bankruptcy." *Journal of Accounting Research* (Spring 1980), pp. 109–31.

Phillips, Lawrence C. "Accounting for Troubled Debt Restructurings." *CPA Journal* (July 1977), pp. 22–26.

Pinches, G.E., and Trieschmann, J.S. "The Efficiency of Alternative Models for Solvency Surveillance in the Insurance Industry." *Journal of Risk and Insurance* (December 1974), pp. 563–77.

_____. "Discriminant Analysis, Classification Results, and Financially Distressed P-L Insurers." *Journal of Risk and Insurance* (June 1977), pp. 289–98.

Ratcliffe, Thomas A., and Munter, Paul. "Accounting for a Troubled Debt Restructuring from the Perspective of the Creditor." *Journal of Commercial Bank Lending* (July 1980), pp. 54–62.

Ratcliffe, Thomas A., and Raiborn, D.D. "Accounting for Troubled Debt Restructurings." *Financial Executive* (March 1981), pp. 20–23.

Rose, Peter S., Andrews, Wesley T., and Giroux, Gary A. "Predicting Business Failure: A Macroeconomic Perspective." *Journal of Accounting, Auditing, and Finance* (Fall 1982), pp. 20–31.

Rose, Peter S., and Giroux, Gary A. "Predicting Corporate Bankruptcy: An Analytical and Empirical Evaluation." Unpublished working paper, Texas A & M University, 1980.

Scheer, Frederick C. "Using Statistics to Forecast Default." *Credit and Financial Management* (January 1977), pp. 28–29, 37.

Scott, Elton. "On the Financial Application of Discriminant Analysis: Comment." *Journal of Financial and Quantitative Analysis* (March 1978), pp. 201–5.

Scott, James. "The Probability of Bankruptcy: A Comparison of Empirical Predictions and Theoretical Models." *Journal of Banking and Finance* (Spring 1981), pp. 317–44.

Scott, James H., Jr. "A Theory of Optimal Capital Structure." *The Bell Journal of Economics* (Spring 1976), pp. 33–54.

_____. "Bankruptcy, Secured Debt, and Optimal Capital Structure: Reply." *Journal of Finance* (March 1979), pp. 253-60.

Sinkey, J.F. "A Multivariate Statistical Analysis of the Characteristics of Problem Banks." *Journal of Finance* (March 1975), pp. 21-36.

Solomon, Ira. "A Comparison of General Price Level and Historical Cost Financial Statement in the Prediction of Bankruptcy: A Comment." *The Accounting Review* (July 1980), pp. 511-15.

Stiglitz, J.E. "Some Aspects of the Pure Theory of Corporate Finance: Bankruptcies and Takeovers." *Bell Journal of Economics and Management Science* (Autumn 1972), pp. 458-82.

Tatsuoka, Maurice M. *Multivariate Analysis: Techniques for Educational and Psychological Research.* New York: John Wiley and Sons, 1971.

Tinsley, P.A. "Capital Structure, PreCautionary Balances, and Valuation of the Firm: The Problem of Financial Risk." *Journal of Financial and Quantitative Analysis* (March 1970), pp. 33-62.

Trieschmann, J.S., and Pinches, G.E. "A Multivariate Model for Predicting Financially Distressed P-L Insurers." *Journal of Risk and Insurance* (September 1973), pp. 327-38.

U.S. Department of Commerce. *Business Conditions Digest.* February 1976.

_____. *Business Conditions Digest.* November 1980.

_____. *Business Conditions Digest.* July 1981.

_____. *Business Conditions Digest.* May 1982.

U.S. Department of Commerce, Bureau of the Census. *Statistical Abstract of the United States,* 103d ed., 1982-83.

U.S. Department of Commerce/Social and Economic Statistics Administration/Bureau of Economic Analysis. *Survey of Current Business.* May 1973.

_____. *Survey of Current Business.* December 1973.

_____. *Survey of Current Business.* October 1975.

_____. *Survey of Current Business.* November 1977.

_____. *Survey of Current Business.* January 1980.

_____. *Survey of Current Business.* December 1981.

_____. *Survey of Current Business.* March 1983.

U.S. Government Printing Office. *Economic Report of the President.* 1973.

_____. *Economic Report of the President.* 1974.

_____. *Economic Report of the President.* 1975.

_____. *Economic Report of the President.* 1976.

_____. *Economic Report of the President.* 1977.

_____. *Economic Report of the President.* 1978.

_____. *Economic Report of the President.* 1979.

_____. *Economic Report of the President.* 1980.

_____. *Economic Report of the President.* 1981.

_____. *Economic Report of the President.* 1982.

Vinso, Joseph D. "A Determination of the Risk of Ruin." *Journal of Financial and Quantitative Analysis* (March 1979), pp. 77-100.

Warner, Jerold B. "Bankruptcy Costs: Some Evidence." *The Journal of Finance* (May 1977), pp. 337-47.

Weston, J. Fred, and Brigham, Eugene F. *Managerial Finance.* Hinsdale, IL: The Dryden Press, 1975.

Wilcox, J.W. "A Simple Theory of Financial Ratios as Predictors of Failure." *Journal of Accounting Research* (Autumn 1971), pp. 389-95.

_____. "A Prediction of Business Failure Using Accounting Data." *Empirical Research in Accounting: Selected Studies* (1973), pp. 1963-79.

Index